THE POWER of TWO WORKBOOK

Communication Skills *for a* Strong & Loving Marriage

SUSAN HEITLER, PH.D.
ABIGAIL HIRSCH, MA

New Harbinger Publications, Inc.

Publisher's Note

This publication is designed to provide accurate and authoritative information in regard to the subject matter covered. It is sold with the understanding that the publisher is not engaged in rendering psychological, financial, legal, or other professional services. If expert assistance or counseling is needed, the services of a competent professional should be sought.

Distributed in Canada by Raincoast Books

New Harbinger Publications, Inc.
5674 Shattuck Avenue
Oakland, CA 94609

Cover design by Amy Shoup
Edited by Brady Kahn
Text design by Tracy Marie Carlson

ISBN-10 1-57224-334-1
ISBN-13 978-1-57224-334-7

Printed in the United States of America

New Harbinger Publications' website address: www.newharbinger.com

16   15   14

15   14   13   12   11   10

To our husbands,
Bruce and Adam,
with whom we share
the blessings of the power of two.

Contents

Introduction

When two individuals choose to form a marital union, their decision has enormous power, for better or worse, over the quality of their lives. Their marriage can bring them infinite blessings, or misfortune, disappointment, and strife.

Bonnie and Jack, an attractive, bright, capable, and likable couple, found that their marriage had become a source of ever increasing unhappiness. After one especially distressing evening, Bonnie phoned our offices to schedule an introductory session. "Maybe I should divorce him!" she told us. "I'm fed up. I'm not in love anymore. I don't know this man!"

How did Bonnie and Jack's marriage, launched with great hopes, disintegrate? Bonnie and Jack seemed on every dimension to be a perfectly matched pair. What had gone wrong?

Like all couples, Bonnie and Jack from time to time had faced difficult situations. Unfortunately, however, when they had tried to talk over these difficulties, their talking increased their distress. One would bark and the other would badger. Bonnie would explode, and Jack would back off, "I give up—Do it your way." Unable to resolve differences that troubled them, Bonnie and Jack talked less and less. Tension replaced affection, they turned away from each other, chose separate paths, and grew apart.

Fortunately, Bonnie decided to get help. Jack joined her. The couple agreed to remedy their skill deficits so that they could talk through the divisive issues that had mounted over the years. By mastering the communication skills you will be learning in this book, they hoped to save their marriage.

Their hope was fulfilled. They studied, and as they gained marriage communication skills Bonnie and Jack regained their positive connection. Laughter and affection returned to their home. A rekindled sexual relationship brought them pleasure and closeness. Instead of evenings in separate rooms, now after dinner they sat together on their back patio, sharing the day's events.

Bonnie and Jack were elated to discover that all they had really needed was a how-to course. At the same time, Bonnie lamented, "I just wish someone had given us this information thirty years ago!"

"Better yet," Jack added, "Why didn't anyone teach us these tools in high school or college so by the time we met we would have known how to succeed as a couple?"

"... And They Lived Happily Ever After"

You meet your prince or princess. You fall in love. You commit to staying together forever. Will love alone be enough to keep you living together happily ever after? Or will you succumb to distancing and bickering?

Your best marriage insurance is to learn the skills you need for marriage success. The interactive exercises in this workbook teach you these skills—skills for talking together openly and safely, for finding win-win solutions to conflicts, and for sustaining a loving home.

The good news then gets even better. As you learn to use these skills at home, you will find that you can use the same skills for smoothing out wrinkles in all of your relationships. You can use them to handle sensitive situations at work, with extended family and friends, and, if you have children, to become a more effective parent.

What You Will Learn, and How

You may be wondering if this workbook is for someone in your situation. It is for you if you are currently in a couple relationship, engaged, or married and looking to make your partnership the best it can be. It is also for you if you are single and want to be prepared for finding a marriage partner, or if you are between relationships and wanting more success in the next.

The first five chapters of this workbook teach the building blocks of cooperative dialogue upon which all healthy marriage communication relies. The next five chapters show you how to use these building blocks to manage a variety of difficult but common marriage challenges. The workbook concludes with exercises to further increase the positives in your marriage by supporting each other in difficult times and by ensuring that your home radiates affection.

Each skill is introduced with a brief explanation of why the skill is important and how to do it. Skill drills are the second step. Exercises give you a way to practice, on paper, using the skill in familiar household situations. Each skill drill concludes by reviewing what you have learned, preparing you to move forward.

The exercises are practice opportunities, not tests, and meant to be enjoyed. We provide you with sample answers to be sure you understand the skill you are practicing. Compare your answers with the sample to feel confident that you are on track.

While many of the questions will feel easy to you, expect some to take considerable thought. If one seems too puzzling, move on to the next question and return to the challenging one later.

Do write in your answers rather than just thinking about them. Thinking is faster, but writing engenders more learning. Reading aloud the answers you have written also can be helpful.

If you are in a couple relationship or married, it generally is a good idea for each of you to write in your own book. Using separate books gives you space to create unique answers and to study at your own pace. That way you and your partner can work either together or independently. From time to time compare answers and talk over what you have been learning. The workbook experience then becomes a microcosm of marriage—a partnership of two independently responsible individuals who do some activities on their own and some together, and who can be individuals and at the same time interconnected.

Although the workbook often refers to "your partner" and "your spouse," this workbook *is* for you even if you are single or in a relationship other than marriage. We are just attempting to avoid cumbersome repetitions of "your partner or spouse if you have one." Similarly, most chapters include one or two exercises for you to practice with your partner. If you are preparing for a relationship rather than currently in one, save these sections for later.

What if you want to learn these skills, but your spouse shows no interest? Marriages can improve even when just one partner learns more effective skills. One word of advice, however: Whether you are working on the project alone or with your partner, be sure that you focus on using the skills yourself. Avoid giving in to the temptation to monitor and correct your partner's skill deficits, a sure recipe for friction.

Getting Started and Keeping Going

To get started, you need only to sit down with the workbook plus a pen or pencil, and—the hardest part—to set aside time. The workbook has all the information you need to be able to use it alone. At the same time, to augment your learning, *The Power of Two: Secrets to a Strong and Loving Marriage*, the book upon which this workbook is based, offers additional reading. The chapters in the book expand the brief workbook explanations of each skill.

Solidifying new skills takes practice. Completing the exercises will give you a strong start. Using the skills in real life comes next. Expect to feel awkward at first. Be easy on yourself, and let yourself have fun experimenting. Pat yourself on the back as you note successes—and share your enthusiasm about what you have learned with your spouse.

How will you be sure you complete the workbook? The exercises are engaging, yet sticking with any project through to the end can be challenging. Keep the workbook highly visible, in a place where you can do an exercise when you have five minutes to spare. Or create a routine that includes daily workbook time—perhaps after dinner each evening or first thing in the morning.

When you have finished all the exercises, you will not be finished learning. Keep the completed workbook. Review your learning from time to time. Return to the workbook when you face particular marriage challenges. Use the table of contents to zero in quickly on the skill you need to review.

The bottom line is that you are embarking on what may prove to be the single most beneficial learning experience of your life. May it bring you long-lasting love and joy, plus a nurturing environment for raising the next generation. Learn, practice, and enjoy the power of two!

CHAPTER 1

Talking Directly

When a marriage is flourishing, partners feel connected via a flow of enjoyable and informative talking together. Your body's well-being depends on the free flow of blood in your bloodstream; a healthy marriage depends on the free flow of information. When the tone of a couple's communicating stays considerate and constructive, partners can share very different views, concerns, and preferences and yet feel all the more connected and caring toward each other. Sharing perspectives leads to understanding and to feeling understood. With mutual understanding comes the full power of two—the power of two individuals to create a strong and loving partnership.

In some ways the fundamental building blocks of communication, talking and listening, are familiar to every adult. All of us talk and listen every day, and have been doing so for years. On the other hand, talking and listening about sensitive issues in a marriage takes special skills to keep the dialogue connection open and the information flowing smoothly and safely. The more consistently you use these skills, the more consistently your union will feel strong and loving.

Say It

Communication begins with saying what is on your mind. Holding views, concerns, and preferences without explicitly verbalizing what you are thinking is like playing basketball without tossing in the ball. The game never gets started. If problem-solving never gets started, problems fester instead of getting fixed. Holding back from saying something about situations that trouble you starts you down a path of increasing voicelessness, irritation, resentment, depression, and emotional distance from your spouse.

What motivates reluctance to say what is on your mind? When you choose voicelessness over saying your thoughts, you may be feeling irritated and fear that your annoyance could yield a defensive response. You may also feel that speaking up is unsafe because it risks not being heard with understanding and empathy. Chapter 2 will help you say your thoughts tactfully to be sure you avoid critical, aggressive, controlling, or demanding elements that would be likely to invite resistance. Chapters 3 and 4 will add listening skills to ensure that when one of you talks, what you say gets heard accurately and with acceptance.

What specific methods can enable you to pass your thoughts, like a ball, comfortably to your spouse? The first is simply to be sure to speak up, both by saying your thoughts and by asking about your spouse's. The second is to speak in positive terms, rather than negatives, with requests rather than demands or complaints. Explanations of these skills plus exercises for practicing them begin below.

Change Hoping and Hinting to Saying It

The skill of saying it keeps communication flowing in those moments when you are tempted to hold back from speaking, even though something important to you is at stake. Ironically, important concerns and preferences often are the most likely to go unvoiced.

Holding thoughts back in sensitive moments can be a problem for the talkative as much as it is for quiet folks. People certainly vary in how talkative they are. Some people are naturally reserved, tending to think thoughts rather than voice them, or generating fewer thoughts per minute than others who are more loquacious. A quieter style can be fine, as can talkative tendencies, especially if the two of you divide your airtime more or less evenly. When thoughts need to be voiced, however, in order to impact what is going on, both the taciturn and the talkative sometimes need to remind themselves of the importance of sharing their inner musings aloud.

One indication that a thought needs to be voiced is an unexpressed feeling of hoping. Hoping can mean you are taking an alternative route to speaking up, the route of silent wishful thinking. Thoughts need to be voiced if you want your preference to be considered.

Another indicator that a thought needs explicit voicing is hinting. Hints raise the topic without saying directly what is on your mind. You are hinting, for instance, if you say, "I need to pay bills," when you mean, "Could you take the boys out for supper to free me up for two hours of bill paying?" Whereas hoping results in saying nothing, hinting alludes to a problem, offering at least a possibility that the issue will get discussed. Expressing your concern directly, by contrast, launches full information flow.

In the following conversations, Alice and Bert change their hoping and hinting to more direct communication. Straightforward communication about concerns generally begins most effectively with the word *I*, then details what is on your mind.

Alice is concerned because Bert comes home late several evenings in one week.

Hoping: (*thinking to herself*) If only he'd arrive home when he says he'll get home.

Hinting: Your work seems hard this week.

Saying it: I like when you're home at six o'clock, which I thought was our plan. What's happening?

Bert is hoping to go with his friends to a baseball game over the weekend.

Hoping: (*thinking to himself*) It would be so nice if I could go with the guys.

Hinting: The guys are all going to go to a game this weekend.

Saying it: I'd really like to go to the baseball game with my friends on Saturday.

Hone Your Skills

Change these examples of hoping and hinting to saying concerns directly.

Bert hopes Alice will head up to bed now.

Hoping: (*thinking to himself*) I hope she sees I'm heading upstairs.

Hinting: I'm getting tired.

Saying it: _____

_____

Alice would like Bert to turn out his reading light so she can fall asleep.

Hoping: (*thinking to herself*) I hope Bert finishes reading soon.

Hinting: That light's pretty bright.

Saying it: _____

_____

Say It with I

Notice that straightforward talking about concerns generally begins with the pronoun *I*. Starting with *I* means that you take your own thoughts and concerns seriously and increases the odds that your spouse will do the same.

Later chapters will explain more about the importance of this powerful tiny word. For now, however, experiment with using *I* to launch saying your thoughts.

Hone Your Skills

Rewrite the following responses helping Bert and Alice to say their concerns. Start with *I* and then detail their thoughts and preferences.

Bert is tired of having broccoli every night at dinner. He'd prefer more variety.

Hinting: We've sure been having a lot of broccoli.

Saying it: _____

_____

Alice doesn't like the way Bert tracks mud into the house.

Hoping: (thinking to herself) Ugh. If only he'd wipe his boots on the doormat . . .

Saying it: _____

_____

Bert wants to go to religious services more regularly.

Hinting: Isn't the choir's singing uplifting?

Saying it: _____

_____

Next time something is on your mind, beware of becoming voiceless. Instead, say it, as you have been doing in the exercises above. Starting with the word *I* flags to your spouse that your comment is not merely an observation about the world out there, but is an intimate message sharing your personal concerns.

There is nothing wrong with hoping or with making hints. Hoping lets you know there is something you want; hoping gets you started. Hints also are fine. They serve as an introduction to indicate to your spouse that you are thinking about something. They just don't suffice as a full expression of what is on your mind. Adding an *I* explanation launches full communication.

Change Wondering, Guessing, and Assuming to Asking

What do you do if your spouse is saying or doing something that confuses or troubles you? Wondering, guessing, or assuming you know your spouse's thoughts is similar to hoping and hinting. Speculation becomes a problem if it serves as the endpoint for information flow at times when you need to keep the conversation rolling.

Wondering, guessing, or assuming what your spouse is thinking does little to find out your spouse's actual thoughts. Like voicelessness, these speculations generate feelings of powerlessness. In addition, they invite misunderstandings. Asking, by contrast, empowers you with reliable information. Asking, like speaking directly, initiates the information flow that enables you to stay connected as synchronized teammates.

Notice the improvement when Alice and Bert ask, instead of wondering or guessing.

It is April twelfth and Alice wants to get started on their taxes.

Wondering: *(silently musing)* I wonder when Bert will get his paperwork together.

Asking: Do you know where your W-2s are? I would like to do the taxes tonight. How would you feel about that?

It's rush hour, Alice is driving, and Bert is worried they'll be late to a meeting.

Guessing: *(annoyed)* I guess you're going on the highway.

Asking: I find Cherry Street faster when there's traffic. How about going that way?

Hone Your Skills

Do you assume instead of asking? Practice asking questions. In each scenario change the speculating to a direct question.

The paint on the door is peeling and you are afraid your spouse doesn't want to repaint.

Assuming: I'm sure you'll never get around to repainting the front door.

Asking: _____

_____

Your white socks turned blue when your spouse did the laundry.

Guessing: I guess you don't agree with me about sorting the darks and lights.

Asking: _____

_____

Your favorite band will be playing in a few weeks. You would love to go hear them.

Wondering: *(to yourself)* I wonder if we can afford to go to the concert.

Asking: _____

_____

Begin Questions with "How" and "What"

Questions that stimulate informative answers almost all begin with *what* or *how*. Questions that begin "Are you?" or "Do you?" invite yes or no answers. *What* and *how*, by contrast, invite more detailed and enlightening responses.

Alice: Do you want to paint the house green?

Bert: No.

Alice: Have you picked a different color?

Bert: No.

Notice how much more information Alice gathers from open-ended *how* and *what* questions:

Alice: How would you feel about painting the house green?

Bert: I'd rather try a different color since the green we used last time faded unevenly.

Alice: What color would you like to paint it?

Bert: I'd love to try a soft gray with an unusual color like purple or aqua on the trim.

Hone Your Skills

Practice changing, wondering, guessing, and assuming to asking with open-ended questions that begin with *what* or *how*. Use the first scenario as a model. Remember, you are trying to ask a question that will open a flow of information.

You and your spouse are sitting down to watch TV.

Guessing: I bet you want to watch the news.

Asking with what: What do you want to watch tonight?

Asking with how: How would you feel about watching something different tonight?

The garage door opener suddenly isn't working.

Wondering: I wonder if my husband will be irritated if I buy a new one.

Asking with what or how: _____

_____

You think you discovered an overcharge from the hardware store on your joint Visa bill.

Wondering: I wonder if he really spent that much?

Asking with what or how: _____

_____

You want to do dishes together. You find you're doing them alone.

Guessing: It seems like you assume I'll do the dishes.

Asking with what or how: _____

_____

Now when sensitive issues come up you have two alternatives for launching dialogue. Say what is on your mind, starting with *I*. Ask for your spouse's thoughts with *how* and *what* questions. Even better, do both!

Change "Don't Want" to "Would Like"

How can you increase the likelihood that speaking up about your concerns will be effective? The phrase "I don't want" is a high-risk opener. Negatives invite negativity in return. The odds are high that your spouse will respond with defensiveness. The tiny word *not* that's buried in the phrase "I don't want" carries all the negativity it takes to create a complaining-defending conversation. To invite a more positive response, switch your way of introducing your concerns from a *don't want* to a *would like* message.

Don't want: I don't want to go to the same restaurant we went to last week.

Would like: I would like to go to a new restaurant tonight, maybe for Asian food.

This tiny wording change is one of the most simple yet potent that you will learn in this book. Negative phrasing invites discouragement and defensiveness. Saying what you would like invites enthusiasm and cooperation.

Don't want statements are also less informative than *would like* statements. From the following sentences, guess what type of animal Veronica would like to have as a pet:

- "I don't want something that sheds."

- "I don't want a pet that needs to be walked."

- "I don't want to spend a lot of time caring for my pet."

What kind of animal might Veronica want? _____

Now look at this sentence:

- "I would like an iguana."

Even a spouse who is eager to please receives insufficient information from negative statements to be able to respond helpfully. By contrast, as the chart below summarizes, *would like* statements offer useful information in a nonthreatening package.

Don't Wants	Would Likes
Multiple *don't want* statements seldom add up to one clear *would like*.	*Would like* statements efficiently convey your preferences.
Don't like tends to engender defensiveness.	*Would like* initiates constructive dialogue.
Don't want and *don't like* generate ill will. Each time you use these phrases, you spread a dollop of negativity.	*Would like* adds to the positivity in a relationship, spreading an aura of goodwill.

A word of caution: Avoid following *would like* with the word *you.* "I would like *you* to" sounds controlling; it suggests that you are telling your spouse what to do. By contrast, "I would like *to,*" or "I would like *a,*" or "I would like *more*" invites cooperation. These sentence stems express your concerns without telling your spouse what to do.

One more pointer: The impact of *don't want* can be neutralized by adding a subsequent statement of what you would like. If you hear yourself saying "I don't want to eat dinner at seven o'clock," you can neutralize the negativity if you add, "I would like to eat at six, so we can have longer evenings together."

Hone Your Skills

Catching *don't want* statements can be tricky, especially if you habitually express your views in the negative. Practice changing the following negative statements to positive ones. Make up details to fill in what the speaker might want in each scenario.

Don't want: I don't want your clothes ending up on the floor.

Would like: I would like to have dirty clothes go straight into a hamper.

Don't want: I don't want to watch videos at home so often.

Would like: _____

Don't want: I don't want us running up credit card bills.

Would like: _____

Don't want: I don't want to have to wait for you when I'm ready to go.

Would like: _____

Don't want: I don't want to get stuck writing all of the thank-you notes.

Would like: _____

Don't want: I don't like to eat hamburgers for lunch.

Would like: _____

Don't want: I don't want to stay at your parents' place for the football game.

Would like: _____

Change Complaints to Requests

You can think of the switch from negatives to positives as a switch from complaints to requests. No one wants to hear complaints. Requests, by contrast, establish a positive tone and invite helpful responses. Can you hear the difference in the following two statements?

Complaint: It drives me crazy when the car is left without gas! It makes me late for work.

How would you describe the tone of this passage?

____ attacking ____ angry____ annoyed ____ calm ____ respectful ____ appreciative

Request: I have trouble getting to work on time in the morning if I have to stop for gas. How about if whoever drives in the evenings checks if the tank is getting low?

How would you describe the tone of this passage?

____ attacking ____ angry____ annoyed ____ calm ____ respectful ____ appreciative

Hone Your Skills

In the following situations, fill in the blanks with more direct and constructive responses. Note that requests generally include a *would like* plus a question. Use the first scenario as a guide.

You want to get a new kitten.

Complaint: (at the pet store) I hate that we have no pets.

Say it,   I would love to take that cute kitten home. How would you feel
adding a request: about adding a kitten to our family?

Your stock investments are going from bad to worse.

Complaint: I don't like that we're not going to have much money this year.

Say it,   _____
adding a request: _____

You have been fantasizing about a romantic getaway.

Complaint: I don't like that you haven't read the cruise ads I left sitting out.

Say it,   _____
adding a request: _____

Your spouse orders cappuccino ice cream at night. Last time it kept you both up.

Complaint: It bugs me when you order cappuccino ice cream at night and then you can't sleep and keep waking me up.

Say it,   _____
adding a request: _____

Pause for a moment to think back on your experience in this exercise. How did you feel reading the complaints? Complaints give most people a downer feeling. Did you feel that the complaints would initiate constructive dialogue or that they would lead to a dead end?

Saying concerns as requests usually leads to solutions. What feelings did you experience saying your concerns and adding a request? Did you feel a sense of optimism?

"Say It" Review

The first principle of effective communication, *saying it*, starts dialogue flowing. When an issue of importance arises, saying your concerns in a positive way launches constructive information-sharing. Talking together keeps you on the same team.

- *Say it* instead of becoming voiceless when you have a preference or concern. *Ask* if you want to know your spouse's thoughts.

- *Say it* with *I* sentences to voice your thoughts, or with *how* or *what* questions to ask your spouse's views.

- Speaking up with a negative *don't like* or complaints can be off-putting. To be effective, use a positive *would like* and requests.

- Requests generally include a question, inviting your spouse to *say it* as well.

In the dialogue that follows, Sally and Jose have not yet learned say-it skills. Circle where Sally and Jose are hinting, wondering, or complaining.

Sally and Jose's third wedding anniversary was quickly approaching. Sally really wanted to have a romantic dinner, perhaps at Chez Francais, the restaurant they went to on their first date. One evening when they were out walking near Chez Francais, Sally commented, "Wasn't that restaurant a romantic setting for our first date?"

Jose meanwhile was daydreaming about spending their anniversary at a bed-and-breakfast in the mountains, but he didn't say anything.

When the topic of what to do on their anniversary came up later, Sally said, "Well, I don't want it to be just an ordinary evening."

Jose added, "I'm tired of doing the same old thing every year for our anniversary."

Now put your new skills into action. Rewrite Sally and Jose's story so they *say-it*.

Sally and Jose's third wedding anniversary was quickly approaching. Sally really wanted to go out to dinner at Chez Francais, the restaurant they went to on their first date. As the anniversary approached Sally said,

_____

_____

_____

_____

Speaking up generally flows fairly easily when spouses are in agreement. The blockages usually come up when differing views could bring conflict. *Say-it* encourages you to speak your thoughts also when you sense your views may differ. If you still feel wary, however, no need to worry. As you continue through this workbook you will be learning many additional skills. The full package will lead to confidence that you and your spouse will be able to talk together about virtually any issue without arguments.

Verbalize Feelings

Feelings are like road signs: *Curve ahead. Steep road. Caution. Crossroad ahead.* Like signs, feelings convey vital information about the nature of the terrain on your road of life: *I'm frustrated. I feel impatient. I feel nervous. I'm confused. I love you.* Without feelings you would not know when there is danger, when a problem needs addressing, or when something especially gratifying has occurred.

Label Your Emotions

Expressing feelings constructively depends on being able to notice your internal emotional state and label it with words. In the following examples, the speaker notes a feeling and chooses a word to describe it.

- "I'm *delighted* that we're going to a movie tonight."

- "I *love* the idea of surprising your mother."

- "I am *horrified* at the idea of your friend marrying that woman he's been dating.

- "With this new job, I am *dreading* the coming of winter, because I'll have to work out in the cold."

- "I feel *sad* when we come home from work and Sammy is no longer there barking and jumping up on us.

Emotions such as delight, disgust, frustration, excitement, and horror convey vital data about what is going on in your life. Being aware of feelings and labeling them enables you to think about them, talk about them with others, and deal more effectively with the situations that have evoked them.

Being able to recognize and verbalize feelings plays a major role in how intimate two people feel as a couple. How much you talk about your feelings determines how intimate you will feel with each other. The opposite is also true. The more intimate you feel, the more you will want to share your private feelings and thoughts.

Explore Your Background

To discuss feelings, spouses need to know that their feelings will be received with interest and concern. Skills for listening to feelings will be elaborated further on in this workbook. For now, let's explore how feelings were handled in your family of origin. Fill in the blanks below.

1. When I felt sad as a child, I used to _____

_____

2. When I felt mad, I used to _____

_____

3. When I felt scared, I used to _____

_____

4. When I felt happy, I used to _____

_____

If you grew up in a household in which you talked about feelings with your parents or other caretakers and they responded with helpful interest, expressing feelings probably comes easily to you as an adult. Treasure this ability and use it. If you grew up in a household where verbalizing feelings did not feel safe or welcomed, expressing feelings may feel new and awkward at first, but with practice will flow more naturally.

In either case the following series of exercises can enhance your ability to recognize internal emotional states, label them, and share them with your spouse.

Feelings versus Thoughts

Feelings generally get one-word labels such as *sad, mad, glad,* or *scared.* Look at the following two sentences:

- "I feel hopeless about making ends meet this month."

- "I feel that our budget is impossible."

In the first sentence, *hopeless* expresses a feeling. Notice how some sentences, the second sentence, for instance, may start with the words *I feel* but then express a thought rather than a feeling. If the sentence stem is *I feel that,* rather than *I feel* followed by a one-word feeling, the word *that* signals that a thought rather than a feeling is on its way. As we have learned already, thoughts are important to share. There is no problem with expressing thoughts. However, expressing feelings adds vital coloring to your communication.

Adding information about feelings to your communication is like making a movie in color rather than just black-and-white.

Hone Your Skills

In the sentences below, circle the words that express emotions. Notice that some of the sentences express thoughts without feelings.

1. "I feel that today's movies have too much violence."

2. "I am so pleased that we are getting our money's worth from the car we bought."

3. "I feel exhausted; I'm eager for a vacation."

4. "I feel frustrated that my boss doesn't seem to appreciate my work."

5. "I feel that my work is not appreciated."

6. "I feel excited about buying a new bike."

7. "I feel that snow is likely in the next few days."

8. "I feel like buying a new bike."

9. "I'm worried that snow is likely in the next few days."

The four sentences that begin "I feel that" or "I feel like" actually omitted saying any feelings. The other five sentences each began "I feel" or "I am" and then verbalized an emotion you could circle.

Pseudo–feeling statements that are actually expressions of thoughts can be converted to express feelings. Just insert a feeling state: "I feel *sad* that" or "I feel *disappointed* that."

Below is a short list of words to help you get started creating feeling statements. Use them or choose your own single-word feeling descriptors to convert the following pseudo–feeling statements to genuine expressions of feeling.

Affectionate	Guilty	Playful	Unappreciated
Angry	Happy	Pleased	Uneasy
Annoyed	Horrified	Proud	Vulnerable
Disappointed	Loved	Resentful	Wonderful
Excited	Overwhelmed	Tearful	Worried

Thought statement: I feel like you don't like my new haircut.

Feeling statement: I feel _____ that you don't like my new haircut.

Thought statement: I feel like you rarely hug or kiss me.

Feeling statement: I feel _____ when you don't hug or kiss me.

Thought statement: I feel that we volunteer a lot of time on political campaigns.

Feeling statement: I feel _____ that we volunteer a lot of time for politics.

Thought statement: I feel that the weather this winter has been too dark and cold.

Feeling statement: I feel _____ when the winter is dark and cold.

Communication of feelings creates a full connection between spouses. Emotional understanding draws you together and can help you make better decisions on your shared life path.

Verbalize Instead of Acting Out

Sometimes, instead of talking about their feelings with words, people dramatize their feelings with actions like slamming doors or spending excessive money. Saying what you feel enables you to think about the feeling and about how you can deal with the problem creating the feeling. Being able to describe your feelings also enables you to discuss your feelings with others. Dramatizing feelings, by contrast, tends to block further thinking and bring talking together to a halt, especially if the feeling is anger.

Young children can only convey feelings through actions. Infants cry when they are distressed because they can't yet say, "I'm in pain. My bottom hurts. This wet diaper is irritating my skin." Toddlers sometimes shout, stomp, or pout instead of talking about why they are upset. If they have no words to say, "I'm ravenously hungry. Could you help me get a bagel to eat?" they have no choice but to rely on dramatizations. As their language skills improve, however, most children gradually discover that explaining is more effective. The ability to recognize and talk about emotions therefore indicates maturity. Adults can talk about their feelings.

In adulthood, acting out instead of talking about feelings generates significant costs. Acting out often antagonizes the audience, and it is almost always less effective than using words that explain what you want. Adults are fortunate to have the language option.

There are a few exceptions to this principle. Allowing sad feelings to flow can elicit understanding and support from others, and also helps to cleanse the wounds of loss. Similarly, acting out positive feelings—hugging, holding hands, smiling broadly, clapping your hands—brings people closer together.

Hone Your Skills

Do you tend to act out your emotions or talk about them? As a way of becoming more attuned to when you may act out instead of verbalizing feelings, especially negative feelings, recall the last time you slammed a door shut.

What emotion were you conveying? _____

What could you have said to verbalize these feelings? _____

_____

_____

When was the last time you stomped out of a room? _____

What emotion were you conveying? _____

What could you have said to verbalize these feelings? _____

_____

_____

When was the last time you spoke in an irritable, sarcastic manner? _____

What emotion were you conveying? _____

What could you have said to verbalize these feelings? _____

_____

_____

To what extent did acting out the feelings in the examples above bring about positive solutions? _____

_____

_____

_____

Once you verbalize a feeling, you can talk about what to do and come up with a solution, bringing the circumstance to a positive conclusion.

Feelings Unlock Understanding

Feelings are like keys; they unlock a door to understanding situations in your life. By verbalizing feelings to each other, you and your spouse can use these keys to enter a space of mutual understanding, shared problem solving, and intimate partnership.

Practice with Your Partner

In this exercise you and your partner will begin to experience the potency of sharing feelings. You will need a door key. The key symbolizes your willingness to open your inner experience to each other. Take turns passing the key as you read the dialogues aloud. As each of you verbalizes a feeling, pass the key to the other.

Dialogue 1

Partner A: *(passing the key)* I feel sad.

Partner B: *(using the key to open a door of understanding)* What are you sad about?

Partner A: I feel sad that children go hungry in the world.

Dialogue 2

Partner B: *(passing the key)* I feel excited.

Partner A: *(using the key to open a door of understanding)* About what?

Partner B: I feel excited because I received a bonus with my paycheck!

Now create your own dialogues from the prompts below. Fill in the blanks, passing the key to each other as you offer feeling statements and inquire for understanding.

Partner A: *(passing the key)* I feel _____ .

Partner B: *(using it)* What are you feeling _____ about?

Partner A: I feel _____ about _____ .

Partner B: *(passing the key)* I feel _____ .

Partner A: *(using it)* What are you feeling _____ about?

Partner B: I feel _____ about _____ .

Repeat this drill several times.

The key is a reminder that any time you have a feeling, you have the option of sharing that key, that feeling, with your spouse—and your spouse has the option of accepting and exploring the feeling with you.

What kinds of circumstances in your life have evoked the following feelings? Take turns being partner A and partner B.

Partner A: (*passing the key*) I felt confused.

Partner B: What were you feeling confused about?

Partner A: I felt confused about _____ .

Partner A: (*passing the key*) I felt gloomy.

Partner B: What did you feel gloomy about?

Partner A: I felt gloomy about _____ .

Partner B: (*passing the key*) I felt nervous.

Partner A: What were you nervous about?

Partner B: _____ .

Partner B: (*passing the key*) I felt peaceful.

Partner A: What were you feeling peaceful about?

Partner B: I felt peaceful about _____ .

Partner A: (*passing the key*) I felt delighted.

Partner B: What were you delighted about?

Partner A: _____ .

Talk Together

Sharing feelings as you did in the exercise above usually enhances intimacy and closeness. How did expressing and talking about feelings in this exercise affect your feelings toward each other? Take some time to talk about the experience with each other.

Make It Easy to Be Heard

When you describe your feelings, you have a large pool of words to choose from. Some words, however, will be easier for your spouse to hear than others.

As a general rule, saying you feel irritated or angry risks evoking irritation, anger, or defensiveness in response. Telling your spouse you are angry in any form—annoyed, mad, or furious—is likely to increase his or her protective walls rather than invite openness as you talk. Telling your spouse, by contrast, that you are concerned will sound safer and be more likely to evoke interest. Concern elicits concern in response. Distress evokes empathy.

Research by John Gottman, coauthor of *The Seven Principles for Making Marriage Work* (Gottman and Silver 2000), found that launching a dialogue by expressing strong or angry feelings tends to derail discussions. Gentle openers such as those in the following list tend to launch constructive problem-solving dialogue.

- "I am worried. I have a dilemma I'd like to talk over with you."

- "I'm feeling blue ..."

- "I'm concerned ..."

- "I'm preoccupied ..."

- "I'm having a hard time ..."

Anger-based words may accurately describe how you are feeling at a given moment. However, if you give yourself a few moments to drain down the anger juices, you may find that your upset includes other feelings that would invite a more positive response from your spouse.

For instance, especially if you are a man, you may habitually cover feelings of shame or fear with anger. If you take a break for a few minutes to calm down and look below the anger, you may then be able to verbalize the shame or fear instead of striking out in anger. "I feel terrible about" or "I'm anxious that" can be particularly effective openers.

Hone Your Skills

Experience the differences between harsh and gentle openers. In the exercise below, circle the openers that feel to you gentle and likely to elicit a sympathetic response. Draw a line through those that are harsher and consequently more likely to trigger an argument.

1. "I'm perplexed. I thought you were taking out the trash."

2. "I can't believe the trash is here! I'm furious."

3. "This bill is outrageous. How could you spend so much?!"

4. "I'm very concerned about how we'll pay this bill; it's huge."

5. "I'm going to scream. My watch got moved again!"

6. "Sweetie, I'm real distressed. My watch keeps vanishing."

The first, fourth, and sixth statements contain gentle openers, one-word emotion labels carefully chosen to elicit sympathy and concern rather than more anger and upset. Gentle openers pay off. Strong feelings indicate important issues that need to be discussed. Strong feelings therefore indicate times when gentle openers will be especially important so that constructive talking together will follow.

Eliminate the "You Make Me Feel" Trap

The ability to label and verbalize feelings can empower you. Unfortunately, however, you can easily give away that personal power by regarding your feelings as helpless responses to what others do. The sentence stem *You make me feel* expresses this victim stance.

You make me feel indicates that you are succumbing to the mistaken belief that your feelings are inevitable responses to what someone else has done. In fact, there are always multiple possible responses. For instance, if someone hits you, you could think "He must be crazy!" and feel concerned. You could think, "How could he do that to me?!" and feel hurt and angry. You could think, "He is dangerous!" and quickly leave the room, feeling thankful that you escaped safely.

Spouses sometimes give away their personal power with *you make me feel,* out of reluctance to assume responsibility for their own responses. Unfortunately, however, when you use this tactic of insisting you are a victim, not someone who could have chosen to respond to the situation differently, you give up your power to remedy problems. You also are likely to antagonize your spouse, as *you made me feel* blames your partner for your reactions.

Instead of blaming with *you made me feel,* launch descriptions of what you feel with the word *I.* Using *I* makes you the subject of the sentence, the owner of your feeling, and the empowered captain of your ship. "I feel hurt." I feel confused." With this magic sentence starter, you are likely to feel more in charge. In addition, starting with *I feel* invites your spouse to be receptive to your concerns.

Hone Your Skills

Practice putting yourself in charge by starting with *I* instead of *you made me feel.* For example, instead of saying, "You made me embarrassed when you told our friends about my raise at work," you might say, "I felt embarrassed when you told our friends about my raise at work." Put yourself in charge with *I felt* in each of the sentences below.

You made me feel like a greedy person when you said you hadn't had your share.

I felt _____

_____

You made me scared we'll get evicted when you didn't pay the rent on time.

I felt _____

_____

You made me feel left out when you went out with your sister the night I had to work.

I feel _____

_____

You make me annoyed when you claim that you read newspapers more than I do.

I felt _____

_____

Putting yourself in charge of your feelings by changing *You make me feel* to *I feel* helps to keep you feeling empowered. Two empowered spouses can create a great marriage, a marriage based on the power of two.

Summing Up and Moving On

Bravo! You have completed the first chapter of skills for open and loving marriage communicating. With say-it skills and verbalizing feelings you have covered the first two of four basic guidelines for the talking aspects of dialogue. These skills enable you to speak up effectively about your thoughts and feelings, so information can flow between you, nourishing your relationship.

You have learned to express your thoughts instead of just hoping, hinting, and wondering. You have practiced raising concerns with positive requests and inviting your spouse to talk by asking open-ended *how* and *what* questions. You have learned to talk about feelings so that you build understanding and intimacy, and to launch descriptions of your feelings with *I feel* so that you are the captain, not a victim, in your life. With this kind of open information flow, you can feel empowered even when you disagree.

The chapter that follows will present two additional guidelines for talking in ways that keep marriage communication consistently constructive and satisfying.

Chapter 2

Talking Safely

In a safe neighborhood, you can sit in your home or walk the streets day or night and always feel at ease. How do neighborhoods establish and maintain this blessing of security? First, neighbors respect each other's property lines. They ask for permission before entering into each other's space. They knock at the door rather than trespass on the lawn or barge into someone else's home. Clear boundaries around each family's space help the neighborhood as a whole feel comfortable.

The world of marriage communication is like a neighborhood. To feel safe, you need a similar clear demarcation of what belongs to each spouse in your joint terrain of talking and living together. In a healthy marriage, each spouse has sole authority and sole responsibility for speaking his or her own thoughts and feelings and for deciding his or her own actions. When spouses in a healthy marriage talk, their dialogue respects these boundaries.

Trespassing occurs in your marriage communication if you speak for your spouse, saying what you think your spouse is thinking or feeling. Your spouse's thoughts and feelings belong to your spouse, not to you.

This book uses the term *crossovers* for comments that trespass on your spouse's turf, violating his or her personal boundaries. Verbalizing what you think your spouse thinks is a crossover. Assuming you know and can speak for what your spouse feels is also a crossover. Statements like "You think that" or "You feel tense today" cross the invisible but very real boundary between you.

Telling your spouse what to do is third kind of crossover. By telling your spouse what to do—"Pick up your running shoes from the living room!"—you are crossing into your spouse's personal realm of self-direction. Telling your spouse what to do will feel controlling or dominating to your spouse because it sets you up as the tyrant who governs and makes your spouse a vassal in your kingdom.

Safe marriages can be compared with safe neighborhoods in another way as well. In a safe community people are careful not to hurt each other, either on a small scale with littering or graffiti or with larger injurious assaults of any kind. Safe-feeling neighborhoods typically are clean, they have shade trees, flowers, and attractive buildings rather than pollution or ugliness, and they tolerate no crime.

So too with marriage. Hurtful emotional pollution seeps into a marriage when spouses speak in an irritated or critical tone of voice. Disparaging, sarcastic, accusatory, or blaming comments are like verbal assaults. In a safe relationship, spouses talk to each other with tact. The atmosphere stays pleasing when spouses talk to each other with modulated voices and respectful words. In a safe marriage environment spouses are consistently considerate of each other's feelings. What they say is free of irritated voice tones or injurious language, even when they are talking about seriously upsetting concerns.

Like most spouses, you most probably have no intention of trespassing on your spouse's turf or of hurting your spouse's feelings when you communicate. If you nonetheless have been violating boundaries or have been speaking unpleasantly or hurtfully, these mistakes probably have stemmed from naivete. You may not have realized that your crossovers or hurtful words and tone have been problematic. You may not have known how else to discuss troubling concerns.

This chapter begins with guidelines for respecting your spouse's boundaries when you talk. We then explore how to replace potentially toxic words and tone of voice with tact. Your power as a twosome depends on your ability to respect the individuality and emotional well-being of both of you.

Respect Boundaries

Healthy organisms, from one-celled creatures to large nations, all guard their borders from threat. They react when their borders feel invaded. To ensure survival, they must have methods for repulsing invaders.

You and your spouse have similar protective responses to invasions of your psychological space. Consequently, if you issue even a seemingly benign crossover, telling your spouse what you think he or she thinks, feels, or should do, your comment is likely to trigger defensive responses and set off repulsion mechanisms.

Jane: You need more time off to go fishing.

Jane's statement, a crossover because she is saying what she assumes Dan is thinking, can seem harmless and even caring, yet it invites a negative response.

Jane: You need more time off to go fishing.

Dan: No I don't. You're wrong. I want more time off, but not for fishing.

In addition to feeling invasive, crossovers are usually inaccurate. Dan responds by trying to correct Jane's misattribution. Negativity builds between them. Effective communication on a subject they need to discuss switches to wasteful discussion of whether Jane's interpretations of Dan's feelings are right or wrong.

Dan: (*continuing*) Please stop telling me what I need! I love my work and I get plenty of fishing time. Stop trying to run my life! I can make my own decisions!

Crossovers usually sound controlling. Jane's crossover sounds that way to Dan. In response, he defends his autonomy.

Dan: (*still defensive*) Are you criticizing me because I've been grumpy? I've just been tired from watching the news until too late at night.

Jane's crossover, by focusing on Dan, also triggers Dan's anxiety that her focus on him will prove judgmental and he will be criticized.

By contrast, when spouses respect each other's boundaries, their dialogue stays smooth, comfortable, and productive.

Jane: What are your thoughts about fishing these days?

Dan: I enjoy an occasional Saturday morning on the lake, but that feels like plenty of fishing time.

Jane: It's been a long time since you've taken time off like you used to for fishing trips.

Dan: Yes, and I'm glad because I'd like to use my vacation time for other projects. I'd love for us to travel to some of the countries I hear about in the news.

Hone Your Skills

This drill is designed to attune your ear to crossovers. As you read Dan and Jane's conversations, think about how they probably feel as they receive crossovers as opposed to comments that respect the boundaries between them.

Dan: Jane, you think you know all these marriage skills without reading the book or practicing. You need to start doing the drills. You'll be surprised how much you don't know.

Jane: Hey, you don't know most of these skills either!

Who was Dan talking about? ____ himself ____ Jane

Was Dan's comment a crossover? ____ yes ____ no

How did Jane probably feel? ____ criticized ____ interested

Dan: I feel determined to work in the workbook every evening we're home until I finish the book. I really want to master the skills, so I feel like I'm the best marriage partner I can be.

Jane: Lately I have just been too busy to study, but I also do want to learn the skills. What have you found most helpful?

Who was Dan talking about? ____ himself ____ Jane

How did Jane probably feel? ____ criticized ____ interested

Was Dan's comment a crossover? ____ yes ____ no

Jane: You press the snooze button too much. It's so annoying. And you don't even care how much it bothers me.

Dan: I can't seem to get up without it.

Who was Jane talking about? ____ herself ____ Dan

Was Jane's comment a crossover? ____ yes ____ no

How do you think Dan felt? ____ criticized ____ interested

Jane: I have a hard time getting back to sleep after you have snoozed the alarm.

Dan: I never knew that. I always assumed you just fell right back asleep.

Who was Jane talking about? ____ herself ____ Dan

Was Jane's comment a crossover? ____ yes ____ no

How do you think Dan felt? ____ criticized ____ interested

Dan: I feel sad that I see so little of my brother. I'd like to visit him more often.

Jane: I agree that you don't get to see him often, even though he's just across town.

Who was Dan talking about? ____ himself ____ Jane

Was Dan's comment a crossover? ____ yes ____ no

How do you think Jane felt? ____ criticized ____ interested

Dan: You just don't understand how important family is to me.

Jane: Of course I do. It's not my fault you see so little of your brother.

Who was Dan talking about? ____ himself ____ Jane

Was Dan's comment a crossover? ____ yes ____ no

How do you think Jane felt? ____ criticized ____ interested

Marriage counselors usually refer to crossovers as *you-statements* because most crossovers begin with the word *you*. Look back at the exercise you just completed to see if Dan and Jane's crossovers began with the word *you*. Could you feel the implied criticism in these you-statements? Did their you-statements evoke critical comments in return?

In sum, crossovers create unpleasant tensions for multiple reasons. They feel intrusive Guesses about what your spouse thinks and feels are likely to be wrong. They tend to sound critical. In addition, if your crossovers involve telling your spouse what to do, your spouse is likely to resent feeling controlled.

Talk in I-Statements or Ask Questions

If you don't want to violate the invisible but very real border between you and your spouse by stepping across the boundary that divides I from *you*, remember that any time you speak about thoughts or feelings you have two options.

- Offer I-statements, saying your thoughts or feelings: "I feel panicky when your snooze alarm keeps waking me because I'm afraid I won't be able to get back to sleep."

- Ask *how* and *what* questions to understand your spouse's thoughts and feelings. Questions convey that you care and invite intimate sharing: "What has been holding you back from spending more time with your brother?"

That is, any time you feel tempted to say something about your spouse, pause and think. Remind yourself of the guideline: **I can say my thoughts and feelings with *I*-statements, or I can ask my spouse with *how* and *what* questions. You-statements are out-of-bounds.**

Hone Your Skills

Help Dan and Jane in the following situations by converting their crossovers into I-statements.

The house desperately needs repairs. Dan realizes they will need a handyman.

Crossover: Jane, you should call a handyman tomorrow.

I-statement: I would like to decide which of us is going to call the handyman.

Jane is concerned when she sees the front door was left unlocked.

Crossover: You left the door unlocked.

I-statement: I was concerned when _____

Jane is getting hungry and wants to sit down to dinner with Dan.

Crossover: You must be hungry. You really need to eat now.

I-statement: I _____

Dan wonders if Jane has been grumpy because her back is hurting again.

Crossover: You seem grumpy. Your back must be hurting

I-statement: I _____

Dan has been trying to be helpful but feels Jane is unaware of his effort.

Crossover: You didn't notice all of the things I have been doing to help out.

I-statement: I _____

_____

The next part of this drill gives you practice with the second trick for eliminating you-statement crossovers: asking questions. Help Jane and Dan convert their crossovers to questions. Asking questions invites a spouse to express his or her own thoughts and feelings. Remember that open-ended questions beginning with *what* or *how* yield the most information.

Dan fears that Jane will get lost driving home.

Crossover: You don't know the way. You're going to get lost.

How/what question(s):   What route are you planning to take? How do you feel about finding your way home?

Jane thinks Dan took her favorite comb.

Crossover: You took my comb.

Question: Dan, any ideas what could have happened to my comb?

Jane really likes the new minister at church. She assumes Dan does too.

Crossover: You must have loved the sermon today.

How/what question(s):   _____

_____

Dan sees a frown on Jane's face.

Crossover: You look mad at me.

How/what question(s):   _____

_____

Jane wonders if Dan feels lonely in the city they recently moved to.

Crossover: You're probably feeling lonely with no friends here yet.

How/what question(s):   _____

_____

Dan worries that Jane is getting sick. He wants her to stay home from work.

Crossover: You need to stay home or you'll be sick for a week again.

How/what question(s):   _____

_____

Could you tell how provocative you-statements are compared with asking questions? Given how unpleasant crossovers tend to be, you may want to be especially on the lookout when you are tired, rushed, overwhelmed, emotionally overwrought, or angry. These situations increase the likelihood that you will issue crossovers.

In the next exercise, Dan and Jane slip into an angry interchange, making assumptions about each other's thoughts or feelings.

Jane: You are overreacting by being so mad about my conversation with your dad.

Instead of using this crossover statement, Jane might have asked Dan a question or expressed her thoughts with an I-statement:

Jane: What was your reaction to my conversation with your Dad? or I hope my
  conversation with your dad wasn't upsetting for you.

Help Dan and Jane clear up their misunderstanding by converting their angry crossovers to I-statements or questions.

Dan: (assuming) You shouldn't have told my folks I'm thinking of changing jobs!

Dan: What did you _____

  I would prefer _____

Jane: You are accusing me without even knowing what I said to them.

Jane: I actually just told your dad _____

  What did you think _____

Dan: (assuming) You think I'm foolish to risk my current job security by thinking
  about leaving my job.

Dan: How do you feel about _____

  I have been thinking _____

The more irritated you feel, the more carefully you need to monitor yourself for crossovers. Stick with I-statements and questions. Crossovers that arise in annoyance risk inflaming anger on both sides. One irritated feeling plus one or two crossovers and you have an excellent recipe for an argument.

Focusing on the other as you get angry can even lead to name-calling, a particularly immature and hurtful form of crossovers. I-statements and questions, by contrast, lead away from anger. They head down the road to mutual understanding, which leads eventually to the resumption of goodwill.

Clarify We-Talk

Couples sometimes confuse themselves and each other with the innocent-sounding pronoun *we*.

We-talk is fine if you are talking about shared actions. For describing something the two of you did, are doing, or will do together, using *we* refers to observable actions and makes sense.

- "We stayed up late last night looking at old photo albums."

- "We are packing now for our vacation."

- "Tomorrow we are taking an early morning train to New York."

When you are referring to thoughts or feelings, however, *we* blurs the boundaries between you and your spouse.

- "We are ready for a long vacation." In this case *we* really means *I*. Your spouse may in fact be less than eager for a vacation. *We* indicates that you are assuming that you and your spouse feel or think the same.

- "We use our cell phone too much" may really mean, "You use it too much." *We* in this case reflects an attempt to disguise a you-statement.

When *we* really means either *you* or *I*, the *we* that was intended to smooth over differences will end up being provocative. To clean up we-talk, use the same techniques as for cleaning up crossovers. Clarify which thoughts and feelings belong to whom by using either I-statements or *how* and *what* questions.

- "I sure am ready for a long vacation. How are you feeling about the trip ahead?"

- "I'm concerned that your cell phone may be causing your headaches. What are your thoughts about that?"

Switching to an I-statement plus a question will clarify who thinks what.

Hone Your Skills

Practice clarifying the boundaries in each of the following we-talk examples. Convert we-talk to an I-statement plus a *how* or *what* question.

We-talk: We sure are enjoying a great meal at this new restaurant.

I-statement and how or what question: _____

_____

We-talk: We need to learn to stop bickering.

I-statement and how or what question: _____

_____

We-talk: We are getting too tired to move furniture tonight.

I-statement and how or what question: _____

_____

We-talk about thoughts and feelings blurs the important reality that you are two individuals, each with quite different minds and spirits. The more you and your spouse can appreciate your differences, the healthier your marriage will be. On the other hand, when you are talking about actions the two of you do together, using *we* highlights that you are a couple, which also is very special.

Give Feedback with "When You"

Being able to tell your spouse about something he or she did that you didn't like is important. It's also potentially provocative. Fortunately, there is a way you can talk about these instances without returning hurt for hurt. How do you give feedback about your distress without resorting to criticism or other crossovers?

If you are irritated, you will be at greater risk for issuing blame or criticism with you-statements, because your focus will be on what your spouse did. Moreover, because you disliked what happened, your comments about what occurred are likely to be negative.

Chapter 10 will discuss in detail this question of cleanups after upsets. For now, however, the key skill to learn is how to give feedback with *when you*.

- Use the words *when you* to pinpoint the problem moment: "When your snoring woke me up last night . . ."

- Use the word *I* to switch the focus off your spouse and onto your own reaction. That way, the main thrust of the sentence gives feedback about your experience, rather than criticism of your spouse: "When your snoring woke me up last night, I couldn't fall back asleep."

- These two elements can be pieced together in either order, with either one or the other following: "I couldn't fall back asleep when your snoring woke me last night."

Hone Your Skills

Circle the words *when you* and *I* in each of the following examples. Whatever the order, the two pieces work together to give feedback without sounding attacking or critical. Read the sentences aloud to become accustomed to the *when you/I* pairing.

1. "When you brought unexpected dinner guests, I felt embarrassed by our messy house."

2. "I felt embarrassed by our messy house when you brought unexpected dinner guests."

3. "When you interrupted me, I was afraid I'd forget the point I wanted to make."

4. "I was afraid I'd forget the point I wanted to make when you interrupted me."

5. "I was worried because I didn't know where you were when you left today before I woke up."

6. "When you left today before I woke up, I was worried because I didn't know where you were."

7. "I wanted to smother you when you almost told my sister we were planning a party for her!"

8. "When you almost told my sister we were planning a party for her, I wanted to smother you!"

Notice the difference between these two statements:

- You left me on my own!

- When you left me on my own, I panicked.

How do you experience the first statement?

_____ as an accusation _____ as an explanation

How do you experience the second statement?

_____ as an accusation _____ as an explanation

As we have seen before, you-statements tend to sound attacking. Even when they are spoken in a quiet voice, the *you* places the listener in a defensive stance. In sensitive situations, you-statements are likely to sound all the more accusatory.

Putting the word *when* ahead of the word *you*, however, makes the *you* reference just a passing part of your comment. The *when you* sentence starter effectively conveys the problem without criticism.

How does the word *when* work such magic? *When* marks the beginning of a subordinate clause, which means the information following *when* will feel less important than the information in the main part of the sentence. In "When you left me on my own, I panicked," the subject of the sentence is *I*. The sentence is therefore an I-statement, not a crossover.

Interestingly, you may or may not be able to analyze the grammatical construction. Yet your gut, and your spouse, will immediately feel the difference.

Practice using *when you* coupled with I-statements in the following sticky situations.

You were worried for the rug when your partner spilled syrup on it.

When you _____

I _____

_____

Your favorite tape, which your spouse left on the window sill, has melted into a gooey mess.

When you _____

I _____

_____

Your spouse was supposed to be watching the puppy; the puppy chewed the dining room table leg.

When you _____

I _____

_____

Your spouse forgot to plan anything special for your birthday.

When you _____

I _____

_____

In an earlier exercise we practiced converting *don't want* to *would like*. One particularly constructive way to talk over a situation which has been a source of distress is to combine feedback (*when you* followed by an I-statement) with an *I would like* statement: "When you play the stereo loud, I get a headache. I would like to buy you headphones if you wouldn't mind wearing them."

Imagine you and your spouse in the following upsetting situations. Fill in the blanks to practice using a *when you* to explain your reaction to a difficult situation. Then add information on how the situation could be bettered with an *I would like*. Reminder: *I would like you* can sound controlling. *I would like to* is better.

1. When you painted our room dark green, I _____

_____

I would like _____

_____

2. When you worked all last weekend, I _____

_____

I would like _____

_____

3. When you curse at the dog, I _____

_____

I would like _____

_____

4. When you don't remember to take out the garbage, I _____

_____

I would like _____

_____

Communicating this way requires self-discipline. How tempting just to blurt out when you feel annoyed! Pausing instead to remind yourself how to handle a frustrating situation without unpleasantness takes self-control. If you can pause long enough to remind yourself to use a *when you* statement, you will find that it can work remarkably well for safely giving feedback—especially if you add an I-statement and what you would like to do.

This chapter has focused so far on maintaining clear boundaries between you and your spouse. You learned to speak your thoughts and feelings or to ask about your spouse's thoughts and feelings rather than to trespass with antagonizing you-statement crossovers. You learned to keep the boundaries clear by unpacking *we*-talk and to maintain boundaries when you want to give feedback by offering a *when yous* instead of criticism.

In the last exercise, the positive phrase *would like* raised the important idea of speaking with tact, which is the focus of our next and final basic guideline for talking.

Talk with Tact

Skillful spouses are masters of tact. They know how to avoid hurting their partner's feelings, how to prevent defensive responses, and how to sustain goodwill.

You already have learned a number of techniques for keeping your dialogue tactful. Expressing your concerns as a *would like* and as a request keeps your dialogue positive, which is one vital aspect of tact. Avoiding crossovers by using I-statements also makes your thoughts and preferences come across more tactfully.

The opposite of tact between spouses is toxicity. Toxicity is conveyed by an annoyed tone of voice or by comments that put your partner in a negative light. Toxic voices and comments hurt your spouse's feelings, invite defensiveness, and have a damaging impact on the atmosphere between you.

Toxic words and voices in a marriage are like pollution in a neighborhood—and who would want to live amidst litter or in polluted air?

Recognize Toxicity

Zero toxicity is ideal. Like tiny drops of mercury in a large lake, even very small negative innuendos can have a toxic impact on you, your spouse, and your marriage. Irritated voice tones, subtle barbs, criticisms, snide remarks, sarcasm, and harsh comments—not to mention more aggressive name-calling or insults—are all unpleasant at best and seriously hurtful at worst. The less toxicity, the more safe and loving your home will feel.

Hone Your Skills

To increase your awareness of toxicity, mark on the scale below each statement how hurtful the statement sounds. What makes the considerate and tactful statements different from the others?

1. "I get annoyed with your obnoxious friends."

    ____ considerate and tactful   ____ somewhat toxic   ____ extremely toxic

2. "Who invited those bigoted idiots to come for dinner at our house anyway?"

    ____ considerate and tactful   ____ somewhat toxic   ____ extremely toxic

3. "I find some of your friends' political views offensive."

    ____ considerate and tactful   ____ somewhat toxic   ____ extremely toxic

4. "The mail pile is getting huge. Any ideas on how we could keep it under control?"

    ____ considerate and tactful   ____ somewhat toxic   ____ extremely toxic

5. "Once again, you blubbering slob, you just dumped the mail."

_____ considerate and tactful   _____ somewhat toxic   _____ extremely toxic

6. "You did it again. There's an outrageously enormous pile of mail on the floor."

_____ considerate and tactful   _____ somewhat toxic   _____ extremely toxic

The third and fourth statements above use fairly neutral words and consequently, unless the tone of voice is irritated, pass the tact test. The others each include negatively loaded words, putting them along the somewhat toxic to extremely toxic side of the spectrum.

Next time you face the challenge of saying something heartfelt about a sensitive issue, you can avoid stirring up trouble by being sure your tone of voice and the words you choose are considerate, not toxic. The following ideas can further help you to keep your comments pollution-free.

Convert Judgmental Reactions to Compassionate Readings

The way you think about or describe your spouse can range from respectful to harshly judgmental. Would you prefer to be considered curious or snoopy? The various labels you give your spouse may all be accurate, but kinder words make for a far happier marriage.

Hone Your Skills

Often it takes some creativity to find the compassionate reading. Use your most flexible thinking to replace some of the following judgmental terms with sympathetic words and phrases. Follow the examples in the first three cases.

Judgmental	Sympathetic
Dumb.	Distracted
Lazy	Tired, easy-going
Messy	Full of life, casual about keeping things orderly.
Foolish	_____
Fat	_____
Overbearing	_____
Demanding	_____

Incidentally, choosing your descriptive words carefully for maximum tact is important with children as well. A child who is bossy, for instance, can be thought of as showing budding leadership. A child who hits has warrior potential. You still need to help the child develop more socially appropriate habits, but you and your child will feel better along the way.

Focus on Problem-Solving

Earlier in this chapter you learned to give feedback with *when you* followed by an I-statement, to make your I-statements the main focus of your feedback. In their ground-breaking book on win-win negotiation, *Getting to Yes,* authors Roger Fisher and William Ury (1981) teach professional negotiators an additional important rule for giving feedback: Talk about the situation, not the person. In marriage, the equivalent rule might be to focus on the situation, not your spouse.

When you talk about a problem situation, your feedback is likely to be heard as helpful. If you switch even for a moment to comments about the person involved in the problem, your spouse is likely to experience your words as criticism. Criticism engenders resistance. Criticism pollutes goodwill. Collaborative talk about a problem results in solutions.

Notice the difference between focusing on the spouse and focusing on solving the problem situation in this example:

Criticism: Why do you and your study group have to be so inconsiderate, leaving crumbs and empty cans all over the living room? I'm not your maid!

Feedback: There are crumbs and empty cans in the living room from last night's study group. What did you have in mind about cleaning it up?

Of course, as you focus on the problem—not your spouse—be sure to continue to use tact so that no toxic words or critical tone of voice creeps into what you are saying.

Hone Your skills

What follows are a number of "stinky" situations. By focusing on the situation, not your spouse, you will be able to negotiate even these uncomfortable scenarios with grace.

Your spouse's new recipe has left the kitchen smelling like skunk soup.

You respond: The smell from the soup is pretty strong. What could we do to air the kitchen out some?

Your spouse is wearing an expensive perfume that smells horrid.

You respond: _____

_____

You are taking a long car ride with your spouse and his or her wet dog who splashed in the pond by your house on the way to the car. The car reeks.

You respond: _____

_____

Your spouse left a bag of garbage on the back porch. When you try to move it, the bag breaks, spilling rotten food all over.

You respond: _____

_____

The ultimate tests of tact come when your pulse has risen and your face is flushed with annoyance. These are the times when monitoring your voice and monitoring your language for toxicity matter the most. Feeling angry does not justify hurting your spouse's feelings.

Scan Ahead

Each of us has within our heads a capacity to prescreen what we are about to say. The ability to filter out potentially toxic comments rather than blurting what we feel without forethought saves many marriages from unnecessary unpleasantness. A little previewing can go a long way to prevent tarnishing the goodwill between you.

Practice with Your Partner

Keep a running list of times that you or your partner uses a toxic tone of voice or speak with toxic words. Use the chart provided on the next page. The goal of this list is to enhance your ability eventually to catch toxic voice tones and comments *before* you emit them.

Start your list by looking back together over the past week. Continue to add to the list each evening for the next several days. Who did what is not important here. The goal is not to blame, but to work together for a safer relationship.

Note particularly the moments when only one of you experiences toxicity. Often spouses are not aware that their voice or comment may have been unintentionally hurtful. These seemingly minor toxic moments are often the most important to eliminate.

Make copies as needed of the chart, and fill it in each day until you can go for at least two weeks without any toxic moments to enter.

Toxic comment or tone of voice	Situation	If I had scanned ahead to prevent the toxicity, I would have ...

In sum, talking with tact begins with noticing voice tones or comments that have a negative edge. Remove the pollution in your communication by pausing, scanning to remove negativity, looking for compassionate readings, and focusing on the situation, not your spouse, to solve the problem.

Summing Up and Moving On

Congratulations! In these first two chapters you have covered the four basic guidelines for effective and safe talking. This is a good time to browse back through the exercises you have completed so far, to review what you have learned. You have worked on many skills.

The challenge now is to use your new skills when you and your spouse converse. Pay particular attention to how you are communicating your thoughts in emotional moments, as these are the times when you both will be most likely to slip into less constructive habits.

CHAPTER 3

Effective Listening

In sports, the costs of dropping the ball are high. In marriage dialogue, the costs of not catching information sent your way can be high as well. If you don't catch something that your spouse said, that information is gone. Poor listening triggers annoyance. Rightly or wrongly, listening ineffectively conveys that you do not really care about what your spouse says, and, by extension, that you do not really care about your spouse.

By contrast, listening well communicates love. Listening well says to your spouse, "I value what you tell me, and I value you."

Listen to Learn

Effective listeners are receptive listeners. They listen to take in information, to think about it, and to utilize it. They listen to learn. Listening to learn means you

- are willing to add new information and a different point of view to your own.

- are open to being influenced by what your spouse says.

- give the benefit of the doubt to your spouse, assuming that anything your spouse would say must have merit; if you don't see the point at first, you ask questions until you get it.

A receptive listen-to-learn stance does not mean that you have to agree with everything your spouse says. It means only that you listen first for what makes sense about what your spouse is saying. After you understand the merit in what your spouse is telling you, after you fully grasp what your spouse is attempting to convey, then comes the time for you to take a turn again as the speaker and add your perspective.

Listening to learn does not necessarily mean yielding to your spouse. To be influenced does not mean to be controlled. Being receptive means only that you are taking in information.

The alternative to listening to learn is listening to reject. Ineffective listening focuses on what to push away. If your first response to something your spouse says is disagreement, pointing out what is wrong with what you heard, you are not listening to learn. If, as you listen, you are telling yourself what you think your spouse *really* feels, as opposed to taking what your spouse is saying as reliable information, you are not listening to learn. If you are defending yourself rather than seeking to digest the information coming your way, you are not listening to learn.

Why do you—and all of us—sometimes listen ineffectively? Listening without learning, without taking in new information, is most likely to occur when you are

- tired or hungry

- irritated, angry, or upset

- preoccupied with a thought of your own

- viewing the situation very differently from what you are hearing

- feeling criticized by what you hear and therefore defending against it

- feeling blamed, shamed, or guilty about what you hear

- not trusting the person who is talking

Explore Your Background

People sometimes lock into habits of listening without learning. If ineffective listening has been your pattern, where may your habits have come from?

- You may believe that you know better, that you are smarter, that you are right and others are wrong.

- You may have learned to reject what you hear because you had parents who modeled oppositional listening.

- You may have learned from being a debater or from growing up in an argumentative culture to listen for what is wrong.

Which of these or other factors might have influenced your listening style? With hindsight, when in your past can you see this has been your pattern of listening?

_____

_____

Whatever its sources, listening without absorbing what you hear creates frustrations in a marriage. Rejecting what your spouse tells you frays your loving connection.

Listen Cooperatively

When both you and your spouse are listening to learn, the tone of your conversation will feel cooperative. Listening to take in information maintains a sense of being on the same team. Listening to reject, by contrast, makes communication feel adversarial, as if you were on opposing teams.

Hone Your Skills

The following chart lists multiple ways that cooperative and adversarial listening differ. To increase your awareness of your listening patterns, think about a recent important conversation you had with your spouse. As you read the chart, check the boxes next to descriptions of what you experienced.

Cooperative Listening	I experienced this	Adversarial Listening	I experienced this
1. I learned new ideas from my spouse.		1. I heard the words, but didn't learn much; nothing changed my views	
2. A lot made sense in what my spouse said.		2. I heard wrong ideas in what my spouse said and spoke up about these.	
3. I added my spouse's views to my prior way of thinking.		3. What my spouse said didn't fit with my way of thinking.	
4. I tried to understand my spouse's different ideas.		4. I rejected comments from my spouse that differed from my beliefs.	
5. I focused on what my spouse was saying.		5. While my spouse was talking, I thought about how I would respond.	
6. I found the conversation interesting.		6. What my spouse was saying didn't interest me that much.	
7. I trusted what my spouse was saying.		7. I was defensive, skeptical, or suspicious of my spouse.	

Cooperative Listening	I experienced this	Adversarial Listening	I experienced this
8. I asked questions when something was unclear.		8. I felt annoyed with what my spouse said didn't make sense.	
9. Our dialogue felt pleasant, stimulating, engaging.		9. I found the conversation frustrating.	
10. Talking brought us together.		10. Talking brought on an argument or left us feeling distant from each other.	

Using the chart you have just completed, pinpoint how and why the following conversation snippets illustrate cooperative or adversarial listening:

Olga: I love reading long novels.

Neville: No you don't; I never see you reading.

_____ Cooperative listening _____ Adversarial listening

What makes this stance? (Write in the relevant numbers of items from the cooperative versus adversarial listening chart.) _____

Matthew: Babies' noses shouldn't run that much.

Monica: Hers sure is running. Do you think one of us should take her to a doctor?

_____ Cooperative listening _____ Adversarial listening

What makes this stance? _____

Heidi: If you bake fish at a high temperature, say 450 degrees, it stays moist.

Henry: There you go, correcting me again.

_____ Cooperative listening _____ Adversarial listening

What makes this stance? _____

In sum, rejecting what you hear creates an oppositional tone. Listening to take in new information, by contrast, creates an atmosphere of cooperation and a feeling of partnership.

Understand the Power of "But"

Rejecting information instead of absorbing it often is signaled with the word *but*. The word *but* brushes aside what was just said like a hockey goalie's stick knocks away a puck. A goalie tries not to let the other team's shots enter his or her goal. A "butting" listener tries not to let the other person's information enter into his or her brain. *But* deflects or pushes aside whatever has just been said.

But is an amazingly powerful little word—and often inadvertently so. Most people who frequently use the word *but* are not aware of saying it or of how *but* deletes whatever was said just before. Nonetheless, the word *but* has a potent impact on people they talk with as in Ron and Sylvia's conversation.

Sylvia: I want to go back to school to get a second degree.

Ron: But that would put a huge dent in our finances.

Ron's *but* throws out Sylvia's desire to go to school, replacing the information she had put forth with his concerns about finances. How do you think Sylvia felt hearing Ron's response? _____

Ron: With the economy unpredictable, we have to be careful about spending.

Sylvia: But I'll be able to earn more with a higher degree.

This time Sylvia negated Ron, brushing aside his financial concerns in favor of her longer-range earnings perspective. In response Ron probably felt ignored and annoyed.

Let's give Sylvia and Ron one more try. As you read, circle words that make their dialogue feel more cooperative.

Sylvia: I want to go back to school to get a second degree.

Ron: I can understand you wanting to return for more school. It does seem like you need another degree to get promoted. At the same time, grad school would put a huge dent in our finances. With the economy unpredictable, I want to be careful about spending.

Sylvia: I agree that school plus no job would cost us a lot, and also that the economy looks shaky. And yet the money would be well spent if I can earn more afterward with a higher degree.

If you were Sylvia or Ron, how would you feel in this version of their dialogue? Connecting words and phrases like *I can understand*, *at the same time*, *I agree*, and *and yet* signal cooperation. These alternatives to *but* herald listening that is respectful, attuned, and effective.

The following exercise is designed to enhance your understanding of the potency of *but*. Notice how much information this powerful little word can toss aside. Remember, *but* cancels whatever information came immediately before.

Hone Your Skills

As you read the following dialogue, circle each *but*. Then cross out the information that *but* has canceled.

Jamie: This week I am going to put up signs advertising my dog-walking service.

Juan: You could, but I think an ad in the paper would be more effective.

Jamie: But an ad is really expensive.

Juan: But you would reach more people that way.

Jamie: But people with dogs are likely to walk where I would post my signs.

Juan: But someone busy enough to need a dog walker doesn't stop to read bulletin boards.

After you crossed out information knocked out by a *but*, how much information was left? Amazing, isn't it! All that was left was the last comment, the comment that busy people don't read signs. Each of the prior statements was deleted.

By the end of this dialogue, both Jamie and Juan probably feel frustrated. Their *buts* have blocked them from making any headway in solving Jamie's marketing problem. Every suggestion either of them made was wiped away by the other's *but*. They also probably felt annoyed. No one likes to be told that what they said was wrong, which *but* implies.

What can you do if you hear yourself about to say a *but*? If you can change your *buts* to *ands*, the conversation will feel much more constructive.

Fill in the connector words in this second version of Jamie and Juan's dialogue so that both spouses listen to receive information. Write in words like *I agree that, and, also,* or *at the same time* to enable Jamie and Juan to retain the information that each of them offers.

Jamie: This week I am going to put up signs advertising my dog-walking service.

Juan: You could do that _____ I think that an ad in the paper would be effective.

Jamie: An ad might work. _____ I'm concerned it's really expensive.

Juan: It could be expensive. _____ ads reach a lot of people.

Jamie: I'm hoping that a lot of people with dogs will walk where I post my signs.

Juan: _____ someone busy enough to need a dog walker probably doesn't stop to read bulletin boards.

Jamie: That may be right, _____ , _____ , this week I'll know more after I put up some signs advertising for my dog-walking service.

With *I agree that, and, also,* or *at the same time*, Jamie and Juan hear each other's ideas instead of brushing them aside. Using *and*, they show that what each has to say matters, and their dialogue stays cooperative. Instead of a battle over which of them is right, their discussion becomes a puzzle to which both of them have pieces to add.

Notice "Buts"

Awareness of *buts* is key to being able to eliminate them from your listening pattern. Remember, most people who use *buts* have no idea that they are "butting;" you too may be butting without realizing it.

The next time you feel tempted to say *but*, use *and* instead. Consciously stress the word *and*, perhaps even saying *and, at the same time* for additional emphasis. For example, "I agree that *but* is a hard habit to change and, at the same time, I'm determined to replace my *buts* with *ands*."

Practice with Your Partner

Over the next few days, work with your partner to notice when you and those around you use *but*. List each *but* in the space below.

Hints: You may find it helpful to continue your list in a small notebook you can carry with you during the day. Be advised that hearing others' *buts* is almost always easier than noting your own.

Buts at Home	*Buts* at Work
1.	1.
2.	2.
3.	3.
4.	4.
5.	5.

Talk Together

The above exercise is both a *but* self-awareness activity and an activity for sensitizing you to what you experience when others reject what you say. As you and your spouse increase your awareness through this exercise, discuss what you've learned, especially about how to listen to each other.

A *but* habit can be remarkably persistent. At the same time, clearing out your *buts* can go a long way toward eliminating irritable interactions. Changing *buts* to *ands* is probably the most direct route to converting a prickly relationship into a smooth one.

Choose Listening over Defending

Defending against onslaughts seems to be in our hardwiring. No one wants to be maligned. If you hear yourself saying something like "I did not . . . !" or "How can you say that to me when I just . . . !", these responses are signs that you are putting up defensive walls. The downside to defensive walls, however, is that while they may prevent hurtful comments from entering, they also block out potentially useful new information. Listening to learn will generally be more effective than defensive responses.

Explore Your Background

The following questions will help you reflect on when you may be particularly at risk for defensive by disagreeing, instead of listening to learn.

Think about the family you grew up in. Who did you feel tended to criticize you? How did you respond to them? _____

_____

_____

How do you respond when your spouse says something that sounds critical? _____

_____

_____

To what extent do you listen to learn at these times? _____

_____

_____

What is the main advice you would give yourself in this regard? _____

_____

_____

Exceptions to the Rule

While listen to learn is generally a helpful guideline, there are exceptions. These instances mainly are situations in which you need to protect yourself from toxicity:

- If your spouse is usually fine, but every so often erupts in a quick burst of irritation or anger, you may need to use a detoxification strategy on receiving anger before you can listen to learn. (See chapter 7.) Detoxification enables you to brush aside unduly negative messages so you can safely listen to the useful information.

- If your spouse is a steady criticizer, then at some point the listen-to-learn rule needs modifying. It becomes better not to listen at all to the content of your spouse's harsh words, and instead to say to yourself, "This criticism says more about my spouse than about me. My spouse has anger, depression, or verbal-abuse problems if there is so much negativity." In this case, you listen to learn just that there is excessive negativity.

Notice that, even in the face of either occasional toxic outbursts or chronic negativity, defensiveness is seldom helpful. Listen to learn something.

Digest Aloud What You Hear

Sometimes even though you have been listening to learn, your spouse may think that you missed what he or she said. Usually this misunderstanding means you have given too little evidence of what you were taking in.

Digesting aloud what you hear is a helpful way to let your spouse know what you learned when you were listening. While listening to learn is essential, if your spouse does not know what you took in, the communication is not yet completed. Digesting means that you chew on the data you were given, mulling it over aloud and adding your thoughts on the subject.

Ron: If you take evening classes, I'm worried we won't have time together.

Sylvia: (digesting aloud) It's important to me, too, that we continue to keep our relationship close by having time together, especially in the evenings. I treasure watching sunsets with you, and even cleaning up the kitchen together.

Sylvia picks up what Ron has said, and mulls it over aloud. She thinks about what Ron has said and voices these thoughts aloud. This digestive listening gives Sylvia a chance to absorb the import of what Ron has said and at the same time clarifies to Ron that his wife is taking his concerns seriously.

Hone Your Skills

Help Sylvia and Ron to digest aloud the following sentences. Hint: Start your response with the word *yes* to launch thinking about what makes sense to you in what you have just heard. Use your imagination to fill in details from Sylvia and Ron's life.

Sylvia: My car doesn't seem to be working and I can't figure out what's wrong.

Ron: Yes, I noticed that it began making noises after we drove in on that bumpy dirt road in the mountains. I could take it to the garage tomorrow and ask the mechanic if he knows what the noises mean.

Ron: I can't figure out how we can manage bigger mortgage payments if we buy a new house.

Sylvia: Yes, _____

_____

Sylvia: Even though we had planned to have time together tonight, I'm really tired.

Ron: _____

_____

Ron: It feels like we're eating the same old things every night for dinner.

Sylvia: _____

_____

As you digested the sentences above, could you feel how much you have to pay attention, thinking about what you have heard, to digest aloud? That's real listening to learn.

Some marriage communication books suggest "active listening." Active listening refers to a technique of repeating back what you heard to check out that you heard correctly. If your spouse says to you, "The sky is very blue today," an active listener would say "Yes, the sky is very blue." A digestive listening response, by contrast, might be, "It seems bluer than normal to me as well; I wonder if it has to do with the rain last night that seemed to wash the sky of city smog." That is, digestive listening mixes what you heard with your own reactions, much as digestion of food involves mixing food with your own saliva for it to be swallowed and utilized.

In extremely emotionally intense discussions, or when what you are talking about together is quite difficult to understand, occasional word-for-word active listening repetitions can be helpful. Active listening prevents misunderstandings. In most day-to-day talking, however, active listening tends to feel unnatural and cumbersome. Digestive listening is more descriptive of what good listeners actually do in ordinary conversation.

Listen and Link with "Yes, and"

Successful marriage rests on keeping both of you important. Digestive listening with *yes*, followed by your own perspective linked with *and*, validates that both of you have contributions to add.

Polly: Taking airplanes is foolish given how many crashes there have been lately.

Ezra: Yes, there have been a frightening number of recent air disasters, and at the same time, if we don't fly we would miss my sister's wedding, which I would feel just terrible about.

The example above actually has four important parts:

1. Start with the word *yes*.

2. Digest aloud what you have heard, finding something to agree with in the provocative statement.

3. Add the word *and*, leaning on it to emphasize that you are adding rather than subtracting information.

4. Then add your perspective.

Some statements are likely to be particularly tempting to answer with a *but*. With practice, you can respond even to provocative statements that seem to make no sense or to be blatantly wrong with a *yes, and*.

Statement: Children who don't behave in class should be given a dunce cap.

Yes, and response: (1) Yes, (2) a dunce cap certainly could be dramatic punishment, (3) and, (4) I would worry that it would make these children even less likely to try hard in school.

Hone Your Skills

Fill in the blanks below with the four steps of the *yes, and* formula: (1) say *yes*, (2) digest what you can agree with, (3) add *and*, then (4) add your own views.

Our country would be better off if we didn't have any taxes.

Yes, _____ , and _____

_____

We should eliminate parole and make everyone serve full term.

Yes, _____ , and _____

_____

Anyone who drives should be required to carpool to work.

Yes, _____ , and _____

Accepting a variety of perspectives is a hallmark of maturity. As individuals grow emotionally and intellectually, they come to realize that the world is complex, with most issues having many aspects. To see the world from your spouse's point of view doesn't mean that your spouse's view needs to replace your own. It just means that you are augmenting what you see by also taking in your spouse's understandings.

Most of the strategies for dealing with differences that you will be learning in the chapters ahead depend on *yes, and* skills. Without this ability, every time you and your spouse have differing views, you are at risk for a tug-of-war. If you succeeded in writing *yes, and* responses to the provocative sentences above, however, odds are you are ready to use *yes, and* responses with your spouse as well. Remember, whatever your partner says must have something worth trying to understand. It's up to you to find what makes sense, utilize it, and add to it.

Summing Up and Moving On

At the outset of this chapter, you learned that listening requires a loving stance, that is, a stance that is receptive to what your spouse has to say. The opposite is also true. Listening to learn and digesting aloud what you hear attract loving feelings from others. Virtually everyone loves to be listened to, and loves those who genuinely listen to them. If you want your spouse to love you, listen to him or her.

Many people think of a good conversationalist as someone who speaks articulately, peppers conversations with playful witticisms, or relates stories with compelling style. While there is some truth to the view that what someone says makes for personal magnetism, a truly good conversationalist also is an excellent listener. To be a great conversationalist with your spouse, be sure you listen with genuine interest when your spouse talks. Remember, everyone loves a listener.

Great listening involves the presence of the full set of skills you have learned in this chapter.

- Listen to learn, not to reject or criticize with *but*.

- Digest aloud so your spouse knows what you have taken in; then you can add your differing view.

Especially effective listeners also add two balancing skills. They listen attentively to information about feelings as well as to thoughts, and they listen to their own thoughts and feelings in balance with those of others. The next chapter will explore these two additional aspects of mature listening skills.

CHAPTER 4

Balanced Listening

The plot thickens. To develop a fully intimate relationship, you need to balance listening to your spouse's thoughts with listening to your spouse's feelings. To complete your listening repertoire, you also need to develop a second balancing skill—the skill of listening to yourself, taking seriously your own thoughts and feelings, while listening equally to your spouse's. With these two balancing abilities—hearing thoughts as well as feelings and hearing yourself as well as your spouse—your listening skills will give you a solid foundation for a strong marriage.

Listen to Feelings

In the first chapter you learned about the importance of talking about feelings. Listening to feelings is equally vital. Talking about feelings only works if you and your spouse are able to listen to feelings in a helpful way.

Attunement—noticing, hearing, and responding to feelings—signals deepest caring. In fact, talking together about feelings lies at the heart of intimacy. Intimacy is the sense of safe closeness that allows you and your spouse to share fears, desires, and private vulnerable feelings—disappointment, hurt, and shame. Every time you talk in a caring way about feelings and the situations that are evoking them, this intimate talking strengthens the love bond between you.

Attunement to feelings serves practical purposes as well. Listening to feelings enables couples to zero in on what is most important at any given moment. For that reason, the number one rule of listening to feelings in marriage is to listen to feelings first.

Listen to Feelings First

Whenever you sense that feelings are arising in either yourself or your partner, put listening to the feelings at the top of your agenda. Ask about them. Depart for the moment from whatever other topic you were discussing. Focus instead on the feeling. Label the feeling. Explore what thoughts and images go with the feeling. Then return to the prior topic with a deeper mutual understanding.

> *Sam had been outside practicing his guitar. He dashed into the living room to tell Dora enthusiastically about the new chord sequence he had just figured out on his guitar. Dora's eyes suddenly filled with tears.*
>
> *Sam noticed, and asked gently, "What are the tears about?"*
>
> *"I love you so much that I felt suddenly terrified," Dora whispered. "I was thinking how dangerous your work is as a policeman, and that if you got hurt I could lose you."*

When you notice evidence of emotions arising in your spouse—a furrowed brow, a hurt or quivering voice, or a teary eye—ask. Instead of assuming that you know from a facial expression what your spouse is feeling and thinking—which would be a cross-over—ask. Asking about feelings often leads to the sharing of especially important insights.

Practice with Your Partner

This exercise increases your sensitivity of each other's emotions. Sit somewhere comfortable, where you can see each other's faces. Do the drill several times, alternating roles.

Spouse A: Close your eyes and think about an emotionally charged moment. This can be one of intense joy, sadness, humor, anger, or any other feeling. Allow yourself to replay the details of that moment as if you were watching it on a video. When the video of your memory is finished playing, open your eyes, and share what you envisioned.

Spouse B: Watch your partner as he or she begins to think about a memory. Look carefully for evidence of emotion. Does his or her facial expression change slightly? Does your spouse's posture change? Do you see subtle evidence of tension in his or her hands? Notice signs of feelings also as your partner, with opened eyes, describes the scene.

When your spouse has finished describing the visualization, ask about the signs you saw of emotions. For example, "Your hands clenched into a ball. What were you thinking about then?" or "I noticed you chuckle. What was funny?"

If you and your spouse can notice and immediately talk about feelings, your feelings can serve as traffic signs and signals. They tell you when to stop and when to go, when to proceed with caution, where to turn, and when to yield. They signal you that a situation needs your attention.

Respond with Empathy

Empathy is the ability to understand the emotions of others. Feeling empathy is not enough, however. Empathy needs to be verbalized.

Verbalizing empathy in a marriage means listening so that you understand your spouse's feelings, and then giving evidence of what you understand—that is, responding to feelings with the same listening skills you learned for responding to your spouse's thoughts. To respond with empathy,

- Listen to learn.

- Digest aloud what makes sense to you about the feelings your spouse is verbalizing: "It makes sense to me that you've been feeling unappreciated. I hadn't realized that when I . . ."

- Ask further questions to explore the associated situation: "What happened today that brought that feeling up now?" Asking questions conveys caring and leads to solving problems.

Being able to respond with empathy gives you amazing powers. Joyful feelings multiply when spouses cherish them together. Your spouse's sad, anxious, and angry feelings will diminish when you can listen empathically.

Unfortunately, listening with empathy is often difficult. What kinds of listening mistakes do you need to be watchful for? Beware of

- reacting in a way that sounds critical: "You shouldn't feel that way." "Don't make such a bit deal of it."

- reacting defensively: "How could you feel that way when I just . . ."

- saying nothing in response, so your spouse feels exposed and left dangling.

- thinking you have to feel the same way as your spouse, or that your spouse should feel as you do.

- giving solutions, as if your job is to fix the problem causing the feelings.

Listening with empathy is especially difficult if your spouse's negative or hurt feelings are reactions to something you have done. Staying empathic instead of becoming defensive takes extra-solid listening skills at these times. Making matters even more difficult, your spouse may not always talk about feelings with tactful or skillfully phrased feedback. The feelings may burst out instead, replete with criticism and accusations. That's when listening becomes most difficult, and listening mistakes are especially likely. Be prepared. Plan to listen to learn, digest aloud, and ask for more information.

Hone Your Skills

How might you respond with empathy to feelings in the following scenarios?

Your spouse is distressed about a recent business trip for which she felt unprepared.

You respond: _____

_____

You are talking calmly with your spouse and gradually realize that your spouse is crying, saying "I feel so sad that my parents fought instead of being able to enjoy time together like we do."

You respond: _____

_____

Your spouse is complaining about an irksome person on her bus ride home.

You respond: _____

_____

How you respond to the feelings you hear determines whether talking about feelings will knit you closer together or drive you apart. Responding effectively to your spouse's feelings is especially essential during difficult times. We will talk more about this skill in chapter 11.

Beware of Minimizing or Overreacting

Empathy depends upon responding to feelings by hearing them just as they are. Minimizing or denying that there has been a difficult feeling is unhelpful. Overreacting, as if a modest problem is a disaster, is equally unhelpful.

Your spouse has heard that his company is downsizing and his department may be closed.

Minimizing: Don't worry. Everyone loses a job at some point.

Overreacting: That's so awful! What a catastrophe!

Attuned responding: Sounds like a serious problem. It worries me too.

Why might you minimize? If your parents tended to minimize, or to become critical, when you showed sadness or hurt, you may have learned to hold in emotional pain rather than show it. You are then likely to minimize or criticize when your spouse shows feelings.

Why might you overreact? In a similar vein, if the parenting you received modeled overreactions to upsets, you may have learned to be a hyper-reactor, one who hears about problems with an undue sense of alarm.

The good news seems to be that if you and your spouse both dedicate yourselves to listening with empathy to each other's feelings, you can exchange childhood patterns of minimizing or overreacting for healthier, attuned adult emotional sharing.

Hone Your Skills

Pretend you are Pat's spouse. As Pat relates to you the woes of the afternoon's experiences, practice responding with empathic digestive listening. Beware of minimizing or overdoing your reactions. Just be an attentive commentator.

Pat: This afternoon, after being stuck at my computer all morning wishing I could be out in the sunshine, I finally went out for a walk. Three minutes into the walk, I stepped in a pile of mud. It hasn't rained all week!

How could you respond empathetically to Pat? _____

_____

Pat: Then, a quarter block later, Lucinda, the neighborhood gossip, descended. "Oh, I see you're heading out walking," she crooned. "So am I. What a treat. I'll walk with you!" *(Pat sighs)*

How could you respond to Pat? _____

_____

Pat: After what seemed like an eternity, I finally made it to the park. Lucinda spotted a crowd of people and finally left me alone. Finally, I thought I'd get some peace and quiet.

How could you respond to Pat? _____

_____

Pat: I looked up to watch a flock of birds overhead. Suddenly I felt a small something fall onto my new baseball cap. Sure enough, when I took off my hat I saw . . . I should have just stayed at the keyboard!"

How could you respond to Pat? _____

_____

Myths That Make Hearing Emotions Seem Threatening

Responding to feelings with interest and empathy may seem easy. A number of mistaken beliefs, however, can cause listening to emotions to seem threatening, tempting you to brush emotions aside rather than to focus on them.

Explore Your Background

Review the following myths, asking yourself if you have let each belief get in the way of verbalizing empathy.

Myth #1: If I ask about the feelings, I'll make him or her feel worse.

When have you had this thought? _____

_____

Reality: Asking about feelings is unlikely to make the feeling worse. To the contrary, talk with an empathic listener often leads the person with the problem to seeing a way to solve it. The negative feelings then lift.

Myth #2: If I ask about the feelings, they'll turn into a flood and just go on and on.

When have you had this thought? _____

_____

Reality: Fortunately, feelings are almost always self-limiting. Whether you witness just a brief shower or a longer storm, listening to someone's feelings can accelerate the return of their sunshine.

Myth #3: If I ask about the feelings, then I'll have to fix the problem, and I don't think I can.

When have you had this thought? _____

_____

Reality: Feelings indicate a problem; you are right there. However, unless the person is a child, the person with the feelings holds responsibility for fixing the situation. If you take on your spouse's problems as yours to fix, you may actually undercut your spouse's sense of autonomy and impede your spouse's own ability to find solutions.

Myth #4: If I ask about the feelings, I'll receive criticism. He or she is probably mad at me.

When have you had this thought? _____

_____

Reality: By assuming that all your spouse's negative feelings have to do with what you have or have not done, you may be putting yourself in what is probably an undeserved spot of overresponsibility for the marriage.

If you fear criticism because your spouse tends to blame you excessively, this is another question altogether. Fearing criticism can mean that your spouse has a negativity, depression, blaming, or abuse problem. Get help.

Of course, it is possible that something you have done will prove to have been problematic. In that case, you are best off knowing about it.

Myth #5: If I ask about the feelings, I'll be invading his or her privacy.

When have you had this thought? _____

_____

Reality: There's a fine line between respecting privacy and appearing unavailable. To know if a particular instance is one in which your spouse wants privacy or supportive connection, ask. The conventional wisdom is that men tend to want to figure problems out for themselves when they feel emotional, whereas women want to feel connected and supported. However, in any given situation the opposite can just as easily be true, so ask.

Myth #6: If I ask about the feelings, I might not like what I will hear.

When have you had this thought? _____

_____

Reality: Bad news is generally better than no news. If you don't know about a problem, you can't address it. There is a helpful saying about information: All the data are friendly. That is, knowing is almost always easier and more empowering than not knowing.

Bilateral Listening

Bilateral listening refers to two-sided listening—listening both to yourself and to your spouse. Bilateral listening is like listening to music that comes to you from two speakers. With bilateral listening you can keep your own thoughts and feelings in balance with the thoughts and feelings communicated to you from your spouse.

Bilateral listening, the ultimate listening skill, may be the single best indicator of personal maturity, of marriage readiness, and, when both spouses have it, of marriage success.

Janet: I'm thinking of inviting the Smiths for Saturday dinner so I can talk with Mariana about who we should encourage to run for the state senate seat that's just opened up in our district.

Jonathan: I don't really enjoy it when the Smiths come over. I have so little in common with him, and I get left with him when you and Mariana get started talking politics.

Janet: I'll phone her instead. We can talk just as well by phone. Then I can invite a couple we'll both enjoy for dinner.

Jonathan: I'd really appreciate that. I also would be fine with inviting the Smiths for dinner if we add the Petersens. They are so lively that I won't mind if you and Mariana go off into your own world.

Janet shows bilateral listening by hearing her concerns and her husband Jonathan's concerns with equal volume. Jonathan shows bilateral listening as well. This couple has high odds of enjoying a smooth and successful marriage.

Recognize Selfishness and Excessive Altruism

With two ears you would seem to be well-equipped to hear both your own viewpoint and your spouse's. Yet using this equipment to full potential can prove challenging. Most people at various times listen more to one side than the other.

When you are hearing your own thoughts and concerns well but show relative deafness to your spouse's feelings and thoughts, you are erring on the side of selfishness. Sometimes called *egocentricity* (I-centeredness), selfishness refers to those moments in which you are taking into account only your own perspective. Psychologists call this it's-all-about-me listening *narcissism,* particularly when the unbalanced listening is pervasive.

Joe: Let's eat at McDonald's tonight.

Joanne: I really don't like fast foods. I'd prefer to try the new French restaurant down fthe block. Or I'd be glad to fix up something quick at home.

Joe: I refuse to keep spending unnecessary money on weekday dinners. McDonald's is clean and as cheap as we can cook at home. Besides, I like their fish burgers.

Joe's adamancy may help him get his way, but at an expense. His insistence on a solution that only takes into account what he wants puts Joanne in a difficult dilemma.

She doesn't want a fight, but she also doesn't want to eat fast foods. Her husband's selfish listening creates negative feelings for Joanne, eroding their loving connection.

The opposite listening pattern also can become problematic. Generosity and altruism—that is, high responsivity to your spouse's concerns—certainly can be loving, especially when your spouse feels strongly about a particular preference. At the same time, your spouse is not a baby, and therefore is unlikely to need consistent favoring, nurturing, or other one-sided attention. When you suppress your own preferences in favor of your spouse's, your people-pleasing generosity risks becoming excessive altruism. Over time, the asymmetry of who counts is likely to result in your becoming annoyed or demoralized.

Joe: Let's eat at McDonald's again tonight.

Joanne: I would love a nice evening at the new French café down the block.

Joe: Tonight I have an urge for fries and a Big Mac.

Joanne: Well, if that's what you want, I guess it's okay with me.

If an evening of fast foods were really as fine a solution for Joanne as it is for Joe, then her agreeing to his suggestion would enable them to move forward and eat, and all would be well. However, Joanne really doesn't like fast food. In addition, she wants a relaxed evening in a quiet restaurant, where the two of them could discuss some important decisions they are facing. In this case, when Joanne smothers her sense that they need time together in a quiet place, both Joe and Joanne lose out. Joe may not even be aware of his wife's concerns. She herself has a hard time hearing them and therefore doesn't speak up for herself.

Responsiveness without paying attention to your own concerns can lead you down a martyr path that ends in everyone feeling upset. Excessive altruism is a recipe for depression. Ignoring your own concerns also can result in losing your sense of who you are, a pattern that some call *co-dependency* and psychologist Andras Angyal calls the "empty shell syndrome" (1965).

Occasional generosity can certainly be lovely, so when do altruistic responses become problematic? As with selfishness, when generosity leads to one or both of you feeling distressed, there's a problem. Bilateral listening is missing.

Hone Your Skills

The following two dialogues include one in which selfishness is a problem, and a second where the problem is excessive altruism. As you read the first dialogue, underline spots where Eric only hears his own desires and misses information from Ellie. When you underline a passage, notice what the effect is on the flow and feel of the conversation.

Eric and Ellie are at the music store picking out CDs.

Eric: We really need to add more jazz to our collection. That's my favorite.

Ellie: Actually, I would prefer something more soothing. Maybe some classical.

Eric: Classical? I can't believe you like classical. How outdated. I know that the best music around these days is on the Knitting Factory label. They always seem to be ahead of the curve.

Ellie: I agree that it's nice to have music that's different from the bulk of what is out there. Lately, I've been really impressed with some of the new folk music that has been coming out; it's different and also refreshingly simple. I'd like to choose a folk CD.

Eric: Hey look, I've picked out three CDs already. I don't think we can afford any more than that, so I guess we're done with the shopping.

Ellie: I'd really like to add a few more, ones that are especially appealing to me.

Eric: You always like my taste in music once you hear it.

Ellie: (*sighs and thinks that she'll go to the music store alone from now on*) Well, let's just pay and head home.

What was the outcome of Eric's egocentricity? How did it undo Ellie's cooperative style of talking and listening? _____

_____

_____

What skills would Eric need to use for more balanced conversation?

_____

_____

_____

What would change if Eric's listening was bilateral instead of one-sided? _____

_____

_____

In the next dialogue, which illustrates too much altruism, underline spots where Allie, in trying to be accommodating, in fact hinders the flow of information.

Allie and her husband Alan are talking about throwing a party.

Alan: I would really like to throw a big Super Bowl party this year.

Allie: (*thinking to herself, "Alan's friends always leave the house a huge mess"*) Okay. I know you love to watch the game and have beer with your buddies.

Alan: You sound hesitant. What is bothering you?

Allie: Nothing. Really, I am excited that the Patriots are in the playoffs. I guess I could make a big chip and dip platter and you could pick up drinks. (*Allie then remembers how worried she is about finding time to study for her upcoming exam. She begins to frown.*)

Alan: I noticed you began to frown after saying you'd make a platter. How about if I do more of the food preparation. Would that make it easier for you to have fun?

Allie: No, really, I like the food to be real, not store-bought, and you'll just do chips and purchased dips. I hear that you really want to have the guys over. Maybe I'll invite some of my friends too. (*thinking, "I would like to see them, but we can't ever talk over the blaring noise of the TV"*)

Alan: (looking somewhat exasperated) Allie, I've offered to do whatever, and the more I offer, the more you frown. Why don't I just go with my friends out to a bar instead?

Allie: Okay. (thinking, "Great, now I don't even get to see Alan at all on game day. What a lousy solution!")

What was the outcome of Allie's excessive altruism? _____

_____

What skills would Allie need to use to make a more balanced conversation? _____

_____

What might have been the outcome if Allie's listening had been bilateral, not one-sided?

_____

_____

Your Bilateral Listening Profile

Bilateral listening requires you to be able to integrate your own thoughts and your spouse's viewpoint into a balanced picture.

Rate how loudly you think you would hear your own concerns versus how loudly you would hear your spouse's in the following situations. Score the volume on a scale of 0 to 5. Zero on this scale means that you would totally ignore or deny the information you are receiving from yourself or your spouse. A 5 means you would hear the information with maximum volume, taking it into account with major seriousness.

Situation	Volume on your concerns: 0–5	Volume on your spouse's concerns: 0–5
You want to buy one new car; your spouse wants another.		
You want to move to a different city; your spouse does not.		
You want to change jobs; your spouse likes what you earn now.		
You want to eat later dinners; your spouse likes to eat early.		
You want more children; your spouse does not.		
You want to leave a party early; your spouse wants to stay.		

You want more time with your friends; your spouse wants the time alone with you.		
You want more (or less) frequent sexual time than your spouse wants.		
You want your spouse, who is driving, to go a different route		
You want the house to be more (or less) orderly; your spouse likes it how it is.		

Reviewing the chart above, when were you more inclined to listen to your own viewpoint?

_____

_____

_____

When were you more inclined to listen to your spouse's viewpoint? _____

_____

_____

_____

Which of the following statements are true for you?

- **Selfishness:** I often listen more to my own point of view, taking my views more seriously than my spouse's perspectives. _____

- **Excessive altruism:** I often listen more to my spouse's point of view, taking that more seriously than my own, and suppressing my own views. _____

- **Balance:** I generally listen quite equally to my own and my spouse's points of view, taking both into account with pretty much equal weight. _____

Attunement to your part in creating asymmetries can help you bring your listening into better balance. If you would like to readjust whose voice is heard how much, be sure to concentrate not on what your spouse is or isn't doing, but on what you yourself can do differently.

Beware of Convincing

A sure sign that one of you has forgotten to listen to both of you is when one of you slips into trying to convince the other that you are right. Convincing—or its cousins insisting, badgering (saying the same thing again and again), whining, pouting, threatening, and bullying—means that you are hearing your own concerns superloudly and have become deaf to your spouse's thoughts. You have momentarily forgotten about bilateral listening.

Situations in which you strongly want something may tempt you to convince your spouse to do what you want. Convincing, however, has costs. The result is usually a one-sided solution that is likely to create resentments and to backfire over time.

Paradoxically, when you really want something, a more effective strategy than convincing is to use your bilateral listening skills. Verbalize your thoughts and feelings by saying I-statements. Find out your partner's concerns by asking *how* and *what* questions. Listen to learn, digesting aloud what makes sense to you in what your spouse says and genuinely taking these concerns seriously. Then you will be ready to combine your spouse's concerns with your own.

Bilateral listening sets you up to discover solutions that will please you both.

Hone Your Skills

In the following series of situations, change convincing to bilateral listening . Use the skills you have been learning: saying your thoughts and feelings with I-statements, asking with *what* and *how,* and digestive listening.

His wife says that a hot tub in the backyard would cost too much, but George really wants one.

Convincing: But honey, can't you see that it's not so expensive? You've gotta believe me.

Bilateral listening: I agree with you that we have to be careful about spending money. Maybe I could save some by dropping my health club membership. The main reason I want a hot tub is for having people over. What do you think a hot tub will cost?

Larry left his wife's favorite T-shirt at the beach and he doesn't want to return to look for it.

Convincing: It's only a shirt. I can't believe you're so upset. Just forget it. The shirt shouldn't matter since I love you.

Bilateral listening: _____

_____

_____

_____

Henrietta's husband loves his motorcycle. Henrietta, who worries about accidents, is determined to keep him from riding.

Convincing: If you ride that bike again, I'm going to drive over it with the car. Otherwise you'll never understand how unsafe it is. Sell it, or give it away.

Bilateral listening: _____

_____

_____

_____

Indira's husband loves the big tree in the front yard. Indira wants to cut it down so her garden will get more sunlight.

Convincing: I know you like it, but that tree is going to die soon anyway. Just look at the yellow leaves. Get real. That tree has to go.

Bilateral listening: _____

_____

_____

_____

Jackson wants to have more time to focus on his artwork. His wife is worried about the loss of income and health insurance.

Convincing: If you can't understand how important my art is, why should I do anything for you? My art is all that matters to me. I'm going to quit my job and paint, and that's that.

Bilateral listening: _____

_____

_____

_____

What have you learned from this exercise about the risks of convincing? _____

_____

_____

_____

If you can remember that there are two of you in the equation, you will be able to accomplish bilateral listening. Sustaining this awareness, however, takes practice.

Practice with Your Partner

This exercise gives you an opportunity to experiment with using your full set of listening skills with your partner. Choose a topic that you would like to discuss—preferably one that you do not generally talk about and that could be difficult to talk about. Invite your spouse to do the same.

My topic: _____

My spouse's topic: _____

Before you start to talk:

Review the lessons in this chapter and the previous one. Which listening skills do you want to focus on? _____

_____

_____

After you and your partner have discussed one of the topics:

What did you and your spouse each do that felt especially helpful?

1. _____

2. _____

3. _____

After you and your partner have discussed the second topic:

What did you and your spouse each do that felt especially helpful?

1. _____

2. _____

3. _____

Talk Together

How was this conversation different from the way you usually talk together about serious issues?

Summing Up and Moving On

Most spouses are neither entirely poor listeners nor always 100 percent effective listeners. The good news is that by paying attention you will find that you can radically improve your listening averages over time.

With effective talking and responsive open listening, you are ready for dialogue. Expanding your dialogue skills comes next.

CHAPTER 5

Dialogue Skills

Collaborative dialogue is like a game of catch. Passing and catching a ball is inherently gratifying. Passing information back and forth in smoothly connected dialogue is similarly satisfying.

The talking and listening skills you have been learning form the basis for satisfying dialogue. If you don't say what's on your mind, the dialogue never gets started. If you can't listen to learn, the ball gets dropped.

The ability to throw and catch with consistency is a prerequisite to being able to accomplish high-level plays in sports like baseball, basketball, and football. Similarly, the ability to sustain cooperative dialogue forms the basis for many of the complex activities marriage partners need to be able to accomplish together. Passing information back and forth enables couples to update each other on events and opinions, make decisions together, remedy difficulties, express appreciation to each other, and enjoy each other's company.

When you say "we have a great relationship" or "our relationship is not doing so well," often what you are referring to is the quality of the dialogue between you and your spouse. When the dialogue between you flows smoothly, you will feel nourishingly interconnected. If you rarely talk, the ties between you may feel thin. After tense discussions, your relationship may feel brittle with potential for breaking. If your dialogue feels overly emotional, your relationship will feel stormy.

The exercises on dialogue in this chapter detail a number of ways to increase the likelihood that your talking together will feel consistently satisfying, sustaining a relationship that feels strong and loving.

Braid Your Dialogue

Dialogue that is just for enjoyment, passing the time of day, can take any form, or no form at all. If what you are talking about is of serious import though, the format counts. When you need to share important information, clear up a misunderstanding, or make decisions together, the discussion will feel more constructive the more the dialogue intertwines. What each of you says needs to build on what you've just heard. One spouse speaks. The other digests aloud, then adds an additional perspective. The first spouse digests this new information and then adds more, and so on.

Braiding your dialogue utilizes all the listening and talking skills you have learned so far—say it, listening to learn, responding by digesting aloud what you hear, adding your viewpoint, and listening in a balanced bilateral manner.

Nancy: I'd like to go for a brisk walk together this afternoon; the weather is gorgeous.

Norman: I love the idea of exercising outside after all the rain we've had. At the same time, I do need to go today to the hardware store.

Nancy: Oh yes, I had forgotten that you want to pick up supplies to put up those new shelves. There's a park near the hardware store. Maybe we could walk in that park and then go together to the store.

Norman: Fabulous. I haven't been to that park in years. Let's go to the store first, though, so we can walk without worrying about the store closing.

Nancy: That's a perfect plan. I'll fix lunch, and then let's go.

Nancy and Norman each pick up on specifics from what the other has just said, and then add more information. Their braided dialogue means that both spouses are using bilateral listening—both take seriously their own and also their spouse's concerns. Braided dialogue creates the smooth interweaving of two perspectives that makes marriage communication a pleasure. Braided dialogue is the verbal intercourse that unites two souls into one couple.

Distinguish Braided from Oppositional and Parallel Dialogue

Sometimes instead of forward-moving braided dialogue, the dialogue becomes either adversarial or disconnected, like two parallel tracks. What would have happened if Nancy and Norman had used adversarial listening?

Nancy: I'd like to go for a walk in the park this afternoon.

*Norman:*We can't do that; I have to go to the hardware store.

Nancy: You're too worried about getting those shelves up. So what if we wait another week!

Norman: You're forgetting that last time I wanted to go shop for hardware supplies, you had some excuse too. I'm not about to join you in procrastinating again.

Nancy and Norman talk like ballplayers who are smashing a ball away from each other instead of cooperatively tossing and catching it. They are unable to move forward in their dialogue because each time one of them speaks the other responds by negating what he or she heard. While they do not explicitly use *but,* their oppositional dialogue still creates irritation and frustration for both participants. Tension pervades the conversation.

A second frustrating pattern is parallel dialogue. Like two individuals standing next to each other, each tossing their separate balls against a wall, couples involved in parallel dialogue ignore each other's comments. Like rejecting what your spouse says, neglecting to pick up on what your spouse says can trigger frustration and irritation.

Nancy: I want to go for a walk together in the park this afternoon.

Norman: I want to get the hardware shopping done.

Nancy: I'd really love to go outside in the sunshine.

Norman: The stores open at one on Sundays; as soon as we finish lunch, I'd like to go get what I need to finally put up those shelves.

Nancy: Didn't you hear me? I want you to come for a walk with me! But whatever—you go shopping, and I'll take a walk.

Now Nancy and Norman each seem to be having their own conversation. The two monologues never connect. While Nancy and Norman do not seem overtly in disagreement, their parallel pattern risks creating tension from no one feeling heard. In addition, they miss the opportunity to enjoy the afternoon together. Rather than fight over who will do which activity, and without skills to create a joint plan, each spouse does his or her own thing.

Practice can help you recognize increasingly quickly when each of these three types of conversation is happening. Once you have succeeded in identifying a dialogue pattern that is creating tension, change becomes relatively easy. Even if just one of you switches to *yes, and* responses, converting to a healthier braided pattern, the dialogue is likely to become friendlier and more effective. Listen to learn, comment on what you hear. Then, add your own thoughts on the subject.

Hone Your Skills

Practice distinguishing braided, oppositional, and parallel dialogues in this next exercise. Write a plus sign (+) by braided responses. Write a minus sign (–) next to sentences that subtract by negating what has been said. Write a zero (0) next to statements that seem to have nothing to do with what the prior speaker said.

Friday afternoon:

____ *Barbara:* I'm going now to the grocery store to get fresh fish for dinner.

____ *Bobby:* No don't get fish. We had that last Friday night. How about chicken?

_____ *Barbara:* Since when do you know about menu planning? The fish is freshest in the stores on Friday. I'm going to get salmon this week. Last week we had cod.

_____ *Bobby:* Cod schmod. It's all fish. I'm tired of fish. I think I'm sprouting fins. Chicken with some kind of sauce sounds much more appealing.

_____ *Barbara:* All you ever want is chicken. If I cook, I pick.

What style of dialogue is this? _____

Saturday afternoon:

_____ *Aretha:* I really need to spend some time practicing my choir part.

_____ *Arnold:* If I don't start cleaning the garage soon, we won't be able to fit in the car.

_____ *Aretha:* I sure wish you would sing the other part so I could hear the harmonies. It makes it easier for me to remember my part when I hear it in context.

_____ *Arnold:* Mmm. There are several of your boxes in the garage. I wonder where I'm going to find space for them? Maybe we can throw some of that junk out?

What style of dialogue is this? _____

Sunday afternoon:

_____ *Thomas:* I'm nervous that we haven't started to move and set the tables for tonight's potluck and poker game!

_____ *Theresa:* Gosh, it probably is going to take a while to get set up. I haven't started because I wanted to use this afternoon to finally work on my garden. I'm still not finished with the rose beds.

_____ *Thomas:* I've noticed that for weeks you've been spending all your free time getting taxes done; no wonder you're feeling behind on the garden. How much longer do you think you'll need on the rose beds?

_____ *Theresa:* Maybe an hour or so. But what time is it? Oh, my. It's already 5:30! Where did this day go? I think you're right. I'd better gather up my garden tools. I hate not being ready when our friends arrive. With both of us working, do you think we can get the tables moved and set up in time?

What style of dialogue is this? _____

All these dialogues are relatively good-humored. Still, the oppositional Friday shopping planning, and the Saturday choir/garage parallel dialogue both are structured in formats that would spell trouble in less good-humored moments. Thomas and Theresa's Sunday poker prep and gardening dialogue, by contrast, models the kind of braided dialogue that creates cooperative couplehood. Thomas and Theresa's cooperation makes them a solid team.

Most conversations are not strictly oppositional, parallel, or braided. Now that you understand the distinction between the three, look at the following conversation between Max and Mai. As you did for the previous conversations, label each comment with plus, minus, or zero. Then look back over the dialogue. Bracket segments of the conversation that fall into each of the three styles, and label the style.

____ *Mai:* Max, I really want to talk some about our finances.

____ *Max:* (*working on a jigsaw puzzle*) I found another blue piece. That's just what I need. Now, let's see . . . Mai, do you see where this piece fits?

____ *Mai:* I see that the puzzle is really coming along. At the same time, I've been looking at this statement from our mutual fund. I'd like to talk some about our investment plans.

____ *Max:* Oh, sorry honey. I guess I didn't really listen when you mentioned our investments last night. I was so engrossed in the newspaper. I did glance at the statement yesterday, though, and I was really surprised how well we've been doing. Maybe we can afford to move to a bigger house.

____ *Mai:* I wish you wouldn't go on about a new house. How many times do I have to say that this house fits us just fine. There are far more urgent needs for us to think about—like a college savings program.

____ *Max:* Hey, I found it. I figured out where that blue piece went. Right here. Let's see, now I need one that is mostly blue, but with a little bit of brown on the bottom.

____ *Mai:* (*talking louder, and beginning to feel annoyed*) I really think we should be thinking about saving for the kids' college. I know they're young now. It's just that college is such an expense. If we don't start putting money away, we'll never be able to afford tuitions.

____ *Max:* That's true. College is a huge expense. And it sure would make sense to save now when we can benefit from years of accrued interest. At the same time, I'm also worried that as the kids get older this house just isn't going to fit us.

____ *Mai:* When you say, "isn't going to fit us," what specifically are you thinking?

____ *Max:* Well, to be honest, I guess my biggest concern is that my den space is already being encroached on for homework. I really treasure having my own quiet retreat room.

____ *Mai:* That's sure important. In fact, I really appreciate how you can go in there for just a few minutes and come out so refreshed, even when things are crazy.

____ *Max:* I have an idea. What if we began to convert the playroom into a homework center so my den wouldn't be the only place with a decent desk? Then we could put that extra savings into a college fund, and I could still have my retreat.

____ *Mai:* That sounds like a fabulous plan!

Did you notice how Max and Mai began to veer toward unproductive, anger-inducing discussion when their dialogue was not braided? By contrast, the braided segments have a satisfying forward momentum. It takes some effort to keep a conversation braided, but the payoff for this effort is clear.

Using a braided format in good times increases the likelihood that under stress—when you are tired, rushed, hungry, or angry, when you have issues of major import, or when your opinions radically differ—you will be able to talk collaboratively.

Interruptions, Helpful and Hurtful

Interruptions prove to be a point of controversy for many couples, which makes sense. Interruptions are complicated; they are problematic in some instances and helpful in others.

Julie: I'm looking to find a place to pick up a new vacuum cleaner because the—

Porter: Don't spend more money this month please!

Julie: Give me a break. What kind of idiot do you think I am? I know as well as you do that money is tight. What I was going to say was that our vacuum is dead as a doornail and I heard from my friend Ginny that the thrift shop near her house has several, all new-looking, that they're selling for next to nothing.

The dialogue you just read illustrates the main problem with interruptions. Julie didn't get to convey the important information she wanted to share. Before Julie was able to explain the situation, Porter interrupted. He had assumed that he knew what his wife was going to say and leapt to negate what he thought was her suggestion. This negating, not to mention the interruption before she has made her point, antagonizes Julie, who returns fire with fire. Oppositional interruptions, by leaving you or your spouse feeling less, rather than more, understood, are provocative.

Interruptions, however, are not always annoying or unhelpful. Sometimes they even can be positive.

Julie: Did you see the new dog next door? He makes me nervous because he looks extremely aggressive. I heard him barking when I was walking and almost jumped out of my skin. I—

Porter: That worries me. The new neighbors scare me, and I could picture them having a killer dog who really could be dangerous.

Julie: That's exactly what scares me. I'm so glad you're reacting the same way! I don't know what we can do about it, but I'm relieved just hearing that you agree with me.

Porter has interrupted again, but this time Julie feels supported by his interruption. Porter has been listening to learn, not to reject what he hears. His interruption comments supportively, in agreement, with what his wife is saying. This interruption feels constructive and actually positively energizes the dialogue. Friendly interruptions facilitate shared understanding.

Deborah Tannen's 1990 book on how men and women talk, *You Just Don't Understand*, reports that conversations that participants experience as lively and fun typically include multiple supportive interruptions. These comments add to spouses' enthusiasm as they talk together.

How can interruptions add positively to your conversations? Interruptions can be useful for breaking down monologues into smaller chunks when one of you is offering larger-than-digestible information bitefuls. Interpolations can help you know the other's reactions to what one of you is saying. Interruptions in the form of questions prevent misunderstandings, confusions, and missing the point when one of you is unclear about something the other is saying. And interpolating exclamations that validate the speaker add positive energy to the dialogue—"I'll say!" or "You sure are right!" or "For sure!"

Sometimes when you talk, you may unknowingly invite interruptions, hostile or friendly. The following list suggests speech habits that inadvertently tend to signal, "interrupt me":

- pausing in the middle of sentences instead of only at the end of sentences

- seeming to have lost your train of thought

- talking slowly

- having trouble finding a word, with consequent hesitations

- pausing while your mind tracks ideas that you are not saying aloud

- giving more information than a listener can digest

- offering provocative views

Awareness of when you are inviting interruptions may help you feel more relaxed about receiving them. Reread the list above and circle speech patterns that may sometimes be part of your style.

Practice with Your Partner

Friendly interrupting facilitates braided dialogue. Transform the following monologue into braided dialogue by inserting helpful interruptions, at least two per paragraph. Friendly interruptions can be exclamations, comments on what you hear, or questions to split a long monologue into digestible chunks.

This exercise can be fun to do together. One spouse reads aloud. The other interrupts with a comment after every two to three sentences. Halfway through, switch roles.

Reader: You won't believe what a crazy day I had. Before I even made it to the subway this morning I had already spilled coffee all over my new suit.

Interrupter: Oh no! Did it make a stain?

Reader: It was a big huge splotch all over the shirt. Some lady was walking a big huge dog and not paying attention and the dog ran right into me. Then she had the audacity to snap at me for spilling hot coffee on the dog.

Interrupter: The dog was probably fine. What did you do about your shirt?

Now continue on your own.

Reader: I couldn't figure out what to do about the splotch. Remember I had that big meeting coming up and I was really nervous about having to give my presentation to begin with. Now I was running late and needed to come up with a clean shirt from somewhere. Well, I managed to squeeze in five minutes to run out to a store and buy a new shirt before the meeting. Of course it cost twice what I would usually pay, but what was I going to do? I had to look presentable.

It just went from bad to worse. I was so nervous because not only was my whole team going to be there, but my boss's boss and the big boss were also supposed to come. After running around like crazy to get the projector to work, finally I was ready to go and about half of my team showed up, and none of the bigwigs. I felt so slighted. It was like all my work didn't even matter. I couldn't believe it. I was so disappointed.

Instead of sounding like an endless complaint, with your collaborative interruptions the storytelling should read like an enjoyably braided two-person narrative.

Talk Together

In some families and in some cultures, interruptions of any kind are considered rude. Children are taught, "Don't interrupt!" In other families and cultures, interruptions signal interest. Discuss the conversation patterns in your two families of origin. When and how, if at all, did people interrupt? In what ways did the interrupting traditions in your families reflect larger ethnic or regional cultural styles?

If you grew up with one attitude toward interruptions and your spouse has a different cultural stance, what view of interruptions would bridge both of your backgrounds? What interruption guidelines might you choose for your future together?

Use the Four S's

In addition to maintaining braiding when you are talking together about difficult issues, four additional elements can increase the quality of your dialogue.

- **Symmetry:** equalizing voice volumes, airtime, speech rates, and limelight
- **Short segments:** speaking only a few sentences per speaking time
- **Specifics:** giving details, not just generalities
- **Summary:** circling back periodically to review the points each of you have made

Let's explore each of these aspects of effective collaborative dialogue. They are subtle but potent tools.

Maintain Symmetry

Similar voice volume, similar speech rates, similar energy levels, and similar quantities of talking keep a dialogue feeling symmetrically balanced. If you talk louder, faster, more adamantly, or more abundantly than your spouse, you are likely to dominate conversations. If you speak more quietly or more slowly, with less intensity, or fewer words, you are at risk for feeling dominated.

Matched voice volumes, rates of spoken words per minute, and quantities of airtime give partners a sense of being similarly valued, influential, and empowered. To the extent that your quantity, volume, and rates of speech match each other, your dialogues will feel mutually participatory and the power of each of the two of you in your relationship will feel equal.

Equal limelight—that is, equal focus on issues that pertain to each of you—also maintains symmetry. Talking more about your work than your spouse's, or more frequently discussing your spouse's interests than yours, sets up asymmetry. Over time, asymmetries of limelight, like asymmetries in talking styles, can jeopardize your sense of being equals.

Practice with Your Partner

Experimenting with the following series of conversations can be a fun way to learn more about the impact of asymmetrical talking styles. You will role-play various styles while you discuss a variety of topics.

Practice both roles, partner A and partner B. Talk for two minutes with one of you as partner A and the other as partner B. Then switch so that you can both experience each style. Feel free to use your most dramatic flair to exaggerate the different talking styles.

Style 1: **Partner A:** Loud   **Topic:** A movie you recently saw together
Partner B: Soft

- How did the conversation feel in each role?

- What might happen to each of you over time if your general pattern of talking was one person talking loudly and the other talking softly?

Style 2: **Partner A:** Slow   **Topic:** A moment that one or both of you
Partner B: Fast   found inspiring

- How did this conversation feel in each role?

- What might happen over time if this was your general pattern of talking?

Style 3: **Partner A:** Longer talker   **Topic:** A favorite pet that you lost
Partner B: Monosyllabic

- How did this conversation feel in each role?

- What might happen over time if this was your general pattern of talking?

Style 4: **Partner A:** Animated, dynamic, opinionated   **Topic:** A news
Partner B: Tentative, low key, or hesitant   event

- How did this conversation feel in each role?

- What might happen over time if this was your general pattern of talking?

Style 5:   **Partner A:** In the limelight   **Topic:** What you did this morning
          Partner B: Out of the limelight

- How did this conversation feel in each role?

- What might happen over time if this was your general pattern of talking?

Talk Together

Reflect together on the symmetries and asymmetries in your dialogue patterns.

- Which of the asymmetries above have occurred when you talk together?

- What family-of-origin roots may contribute to your differences in talking styles?

- What might each of you do differently in the future to enhance your balance in any areas that could use readjusting?

Hint: Beware of crossovers. Suggest what you yourself might readjust, not what you want your spouse to change.

Speak in Short Segments

Unless a speaker is an exceptional storyteller, long monologues lower the energy level of a conversation. When one of you talks at length, the other may be interested initially. Over time, however, the conversation is likely to lose steam. Dialogues composed of short interactive segments make far livelier conversation.

Long monologues pose a second problem. They offer more data than your partner can digest. However much you might say when you talk at length, when the opportunity for digestive listening and responding eventually comes along, your spouse is only going to be able to pick one point to respond to. Most of the rest of what you said in your long monologue will get lost.

Making matters even worse, in order to maintain symmetry after you have held forth in a long monologue, your spouse is at risk for mirroring your style by also speaking at length, which only compounds the aforementioned problems of low energy and data loss.

In sum, speaking in a series of shorter segments of one to three sentences at a time is generally more effective than communicating in lengthy multiparagraph portions.

Practice with Your Partner

For each topic, first experiment with both of you speaking in lengthy monologues. Using a watch or oven timer, give yourselves forty-five seconds for each monologue. Then redo the conversation with short segments. This time take no more than ten seconds per speaking turn.

Topic: Discuss plans for a holiday coming up in the near future.

- **Long chunks,** forty-five-second monologues for each of you.

- **Short chunks,** ten seconds maximum per person. Keep it moving!

Topic: How could you include your extended families more (or less) in your lives over the coming months?

- **Long chunks,** forty-five-second monologues for each of you.

- **Short chunks,** ten seconds maximum per person. Keep it moving!

Talk Together

Discuss your experience during this exercise, including the following questions:

- How did each of you feel in the long-chunk discussions?

- What was your experience when you limited yourself to short chunks?

- Which patterns have typified your general style of talking together? Do the patterns differ at different times?

- What changes might you want to consider for the future?

Hint: In those times when you find one or both of you talking at length, consider using the three-sentence rule: Speak a maximum of three sentences per airtime

Specifics Ensure Understanding

Communicating improves with specificity. General statements are fine to begin a conversation, but they need to be followed by specifics to flesh out the details that create mutual understanding. This principle becomes especially important any time you are talking together to make plans or to come to agreement on a shared decision.

Consider this general statement: "I would like us to buy a big car."

Sound pretty straightforward? Surprise. That one simple sentence can be interpreted in many different ways:

- The car should have lots of seats, like a minivan.

- The car should have lots of room to lug stuff, like a pickup truck.

- The car should sit up high, like an SUV.

- The seats should be roomy.

- There should be a lot of leg room plus a high ceiling for tall folks.

- The car should have a luxury feel.

Specific statements quickly clarify which of the many possible meanings pertain: "I would like to buy a car that will seat six people, has room to carry our camping gear, and rides high enough so I can see beyond the car in front of me." With specific details such as these, there is far less room for misunderstandings.

Hone Your Skills

For each general statement, use your imagination to create three different possible interpretations. Then rewrite the statement with specifics that would be true for you.

General statement: I want to fix up our house.

Interpretation 1: _____

Interpretation 2: _____

Interpretation 3: _____

Specific statement: _____

_____

General statement: I want to do something fun tonight.

Interpretation 1: _____

Interpretation 2: _____

Interpretation 3: _____

Specific statement: _____

_____

General statement: I need more passion in my life.

Interpretation 1: _____

Interpretation 2: _____

Interpretation 3: _____

Specific statement: _____

_____

Digest Specifics Aloud

When you are first learning to braid dialogue, you may find that you think you are digesting what you have heard with a good *yes, and* comment, when in fact you are making a pseudodigestion with generic comments like "I hear you" or "I understand." Effective *yes, and* comments pick up on specific information the speaker has said and elaborate on these specifics. For instance, instead of, "I understand, and my preference is . . ." you might say "I understand that the stock market looks risky at this time with all the . . . and my preference is . . ."

Summary comments without specifics such as "I understand" or "I hear you" tend to sound patronizing, especially when they cover an actual disagreement. By contrast, picking up on specifics conveys that you are genuinely digesting what has been said. Using specifics clarifies for your partner exactly what you understand, and what you may have misunderstood, from what you heard.

Hone Your Skills

Circle the responses that sound specific enough, and cross out those that sound too global.

- "Yes, I agree dear."

- "I hear what you're saying."

- "Yuck, that stinks."

- "What an honor to be nominated for such a major prize!"

- "Oh, no! You must be soaked walking ten blocks in this rain."

- "I had a similar cramp competing in last year's race."

- "What about her comments about our car irritated you?"

- "His advice to buy now sounds sensible in this market."

- "I also really need to get at least eight hours of sleep each night."

- "Of course I'm listening!"

- "Yup, me too."

- "Sure, sure, I get it."

The first three and last three comments sound agreeable enough, but without specifics they show no evidence of genuine understanding. The rest of the responses, by contrast, detail specifically what the listener is digesting.

Interestingly, a detailed yes response typically does not need to include the word *yes*. Your agreement gets conveyed by your reiteration of specifics, and by a cooperative tone of voice. While verbalizing the *yes* is not essential, digesting aloud details of what you are agreeing with makes a massive difference in the success of dialogues, especially when discussing issues of importance to you.

Summaries Solidify Your Teamwork

When a discussion feels complex, if one of you looks back and reiterates the points each of you have made thus far, both of you will gain.

- A summary ensures that all of each of your concerns have entered the shared data pool.

- A summary gets your arms around the full picture of what the two of you have said so far.

- A summary ensures that both of you conclude with the same understanding.

- A summary at the conclusion of a discussion increases the likelihood that you will implement your plan of action.

With so many benefits, summaries are well worth a few moments from time to time. Summaries are especially helpful when tensions are building in a conversation, when the energy level is running down, and when a dialogue is coming to closure.

Practice with Your Partner

The following box contains topics you and your spouse have had opportunities to discuss in this chapter. It also contains topics many couples regularly talk about. Taking turns with your spouse, claim a square that contains a topic you've discussed, and summarize the points each of you made when you discussed the topic. Or pick a topic that you and your spouse have not recently discussed, spend a few moments discussing this topic, and then create a summary.

Hint: If your partner forgets something in his or her summary, use a *yes, and* to add information for a more complete summary.

A movie you've seen	Household finances	Extended family	An event in the news
Fond memories	A moment of inspiration	What you did during the day	A big decision you'll need to make together
Children	Weekend plans	A favorite pet that you lost	Holiday celebrations

A few sentences of summary can make all the difference between a conversation that ends in misunderstandings and one that concludes with full mutual understanding. Most important, the emerging shared view enhances your feeling of being partners.

Establish Climate Controls

If you want to keep your dialogue collaborative and constructive, you need to be able to keep your feelings centered in a temperate emotional zone, away from extremes of emotional arousal. Dialogue proceeds most smoothly and safely at room temperature. As emotions heat up, dialogue is likely to get increasingly stormy. Communication skills will give way to crossovers, criticism, and poor listening. Arguments easily erupt.

Problematic heat in a conversation usually shows up initially as irritation, then as increasingly loud voices, a harsh tone, annoyance, anger, and hurtful words. As a conversation heats up, its goal tends to shift from attaining mutual understanding to winning by wounding.

Effective climate controls enable you to stay inside the emotional zones within which you can sustain the guidelines for effective communicating.

Assess Your Emotional Climate

A first step toward keeping your relationship at a comfortable temperature is to become aware of the general climate in your home and how it varies. What is the emotional climate in your home? Cloudy with a chance of rain? Stormy and hot? Comfortably warm? Freezing cold? Rate how often these conditions occur in your home.

How often does your home get overheated with anger?

____ Almost always   ____ Daily   ____ Weekly   ____ Almost never

How often is your house stormy?

____ Almost always   ____ Daily   ____ Weekly   ____ Almost never

How often is it calm?

____ Almost never   ____ Weekly   ____ Daily   ____ Almost always

How often is it sunny?

____ Almost never   ____ Weekly   ____ Daily   ____ Almost always

The further you placed your answers to the right on the frequency options, the more successful you are likely to be in keeping your communication safe and the atmosphere in your relationship loving.

If your responses tilted to the left side on the frequencies, you need to be especially attuned to the emotional climate-control skills that follow. The skills for dealing with anger in chapters 6 and 7 will also help you to regulate your marriage environment.

Delete "Always" and "Never"

Like starting sentences with *you* or responding with *but*, certain words and phrases consistently trigger heat increases. Look at these two sentences:

- "I always have to clean up after the dog."

- "You never give me compliments, even when I look especially nice."

The words *always* and *never* are worth removing from your vocabulary list. Less extreme words can usually do the same job without being so provocative. Most people can hear most of the following words without feeling provoked. Check off those that would make safe replacements for *always* and *never* in your household.

____ Sometimes   ____ Seldom   ____ Often

____ Generally   ____ Rarely   ____ Occasionally

Hone Your Skills

How might you rewrite the following sentences to avoid inflammations from all-or-nothing words?

1. I always end up last to sit down to meals. No one helps me put out the food.

_____

_____

2. You never turn off lights when you leave a room.

_____

_____

3. I never get to hold the remote so we always just watch the TV programs you like.

_____

_____

Change "Should" to "Could"

Should boxes people in. When we feel boxed in or trapped, we tend to feel agitated. *Could,* by contrast, opens up options.

Should also brings a cloud of guilt and a climate of obligation to the issues you are discussing. *Could* carries the fresh air of freedom to make choices.

- "I should work more overtime so we will have more money for Christmas gifts this year."

- "I could work more overtime so we will have more money for Christmas gifts this year."

As you read the examples above, could you feel the pressure *should* engenders? Did you relax and even feel upbeat in response to the same thought expressed with *could?* Just change "sh" to "c" and feel the sun emerge.

Hone Your Skills

As you read each of the following sentences, pause to decide if you experience the statement as presenting a pressure or an opportunity.

- "I should stick to my diet."   ____ pressure ____ opportunity

- "I could grow vegetables in the garden."   ____ pressure ____ opportunity

- "You should iron the clothes instead of
  leaving them wrinkled."   ____ pressure ____ opportunity

- "I could be better humored in the mornings."   ____ pressure ____ opportunity

- "You should insure your wedding ring."   ____ pressure ____ opportunity

- "I could learn to cook something other
  than pasta."   ____ pressure ____ opportunity

- "You should be better humored in the
  mornings."   ____ pressure ____ opportunity

- "I could iron the clothes instead of leaving ___ pressure ___ opportunity
  them wrinkled."

- "You could insure your wedding ring."   ___ pressure ___ opportunity

- "You should learn to cook more than pasta." ___ pressure ___ opportunity

Did you find that *should* conveyed a negative feeling of pressure, while *could* suggested a positive sense of opportunity? People vary in their sensitivity to *should,* but most feel at least a subtle additional sense of pressure.

Telling yourself that you *should* can feel needlessly burdensome. Telling your partner that he or she *should* is likely to feel downright provocative. *Should* crossovers are especially worth avoiding if you want to keep the climate comfortable. Save your *shoulds* for those rare moments when there is a moral issue at stake.

Monitor for Speed and Volume

Earlier in this chapter, exercises on symmetry in dialogue enhanced your awareness of speech speed and volume. These issues also have important safety implications.

The faster you drive your car, the more likely you are to spin out of control. The faster you talk, the more likely that you will lose control of your communication skills and end up with damage to your relationship.

The louder the music on your radio, the more it will hype you up. The louder your voices become when you and your spouse talk, especially about important issues, the more likely you are to become agitated. From agitation comes irritation. From irritation comes excessive emotional intensities. With excessive emotions, dialogue turns dangerous.

Note Hunger, Fatigue, Overload, Rushing, and Illness

Siblings predictably squabble before dinner or before bedtime. Adults also are typically more likely to become argumentative when they are hungry or tired. Realistically, you will be more emotionally resilient and will use your communication skills more effectively when you are well fed and well rested.

How can this reality help you maintain calm in your home? If you hear irritability creeping into your attitude, ask yourself, "Am I getting hungry? Am I tired?" If the answers are yes, discontinue talking for the time being. Eat something, or sleep.

Prevention policies can help as well. Establish rules like, no talking about important issues before dinner or after nine o'clock at night.

Add several more questions: "Am I overloaded right now, with too much happening at once?" "Am I under time pressure, or feeling rushed?" "Is this a premenstrual time of the month?" "Could I be getting ill?"

If the answer to any of these stress or illness questions is yes, transfer your emotions from automatic pilot to manual control to cool yourself down. Then plan a way to simplify your situation. Reduce what you are handling to a level you can manage without escalations.

Hone Your Skills

Think back on the last time you became argumentative. Make a check next to each factor that may have impacted your level of emotional resilience.

| ____ Hungry | ____ Overloaded | ____ PMS |
| ____ Tired | ____ Rushed | ____ Getting ill |

Master the Pause

To return your emotional climate to the comfort zone, when you note that you or your spouse is beginning to overheat, take a brief cooling pause.

One pause strategy is to change the topic briefly, especially to a topic that is more lighthearted and about which you are sure to agree.

Another strategy is to breathe deeply. Breathing deeply relaxes you. Focusing on your breathing additionally distracts you for a moment from the thought that upset you.

Alternatively, excuse yourself for a moment to go get a drink of water. Water has a cooling effect which may help. Going for water removes you from a situation that's getting too heated. Plus it gives you something to do while your adrenaline levels diminish.

Talk Together

When do you adjust the thermostat in your home? Most people turn the heat slightly up or down in response to only a degree or two of deviation. Implementing emotional climate controls, such as pauses, works best if you similarly make adjustments at the first signs of departure from your most comfortable zone.

Taking a pause signals that you are feeling too much heat. If you know each other's pause styles, you both will be less likely to feel confused or distressed when one of you takes a few moments away from a stressful discussion.

What subtle signs of heat might indicate that one or both of you could benefit from a pause? How long a pause do you think each of you would need before you resume the discussion?

Disengagement and Reengagement Routines

Sometimes a brief pause isn't sufficient to calm yourself enough to resume effective collaborative braided dialogue. In this case, it is well worth your while to immediately follow the fundamental rule of keeping the climate calm:

Remove yourself from a situation you can't handle.

Plan to return only after you feel calm. Wait to resume talking about sensitive issues until you feel comfortable that your spouse is also calm again.

As with pauses, exit routines work best when they have been choreographed by the two of you with mutual agreement. That way, as soon as either of you begins to feel heated, you will both turn away from each other and go to your prearranged separate areas. Neither of you will feel like your spouse is turning his or her back on the other—because both of you will be turning away simultaneously from the heat.

While you are separated, each of you is responsible for self-soothing, that is, for calming yourself down. *Do not* ruminate on what the other did "wrong." That line of thinking will only keep you worked up. Instead, distract yourself by doing something different—read a book or magazine, exercise for a bit, wash your face, clean up a room, do laundry, call a friend. When your adrenaline rush subsides, think again about the dilemma. With cooler emotions and a broadened perspective, you hopefully will be able to expand your view of what happened, seeing your role and outside factors, rather than just what your spouse "did to you."

When you feel calm enough to reengage, rather than immediately returning to the testy topic, feel out the waters by talking about something safe—the weather, a program on TV, or something that has pleased you. When you are clear that both of you are back in a friendly mode, then it's safe to consider restarting the important discussion.

Practice with Your Partner

Work together to create a disengagement and reengagement routine. Work your way down the list of questions, discussing each one together. Put a check in response to each question that you feel you have answered with a plan that will work for both of you.

EXIT and REENTRY Plan	Me	You
Sign. How will you know you need a time-out?		
Signal. How will you signal that you need a time-out to calm down? Hint: A nonverbal signal is often best.		
Space. Where will you each go to cool down? Hint: Go to separate rooms.		
Soothing. What will you do there to calm yourself down? What activities do you enjoy doing alone?		
Analysis. Once you feel calmer, what can you think about to understand what happened? Hint: Your job is to focus on *you*, or on situational factors like fatigue or rushing that made for heat. Do not ruminate about what your spouse did wrong!		
Temperature assessment. How will you know that you are feeling calmed enough to be ready to reengage? How will you know your spouse is ready?		
Reconnect. What would be safe topics for you to talk about before you return to the heated topic?		
Return to the topic. When will be a good time to return to the sensitive topic? Choose a time when both of you will be relaxed, not rushed or stressed, and not hungry or tired.		

A brief pause when you first notice small skill slippages or several degrees of rising emotional heat can return you to a comfortable emotional zone. When would you implement a full exit? The sooner the better for most couples. If a pause is insufficient and bickering is beginning, it is time to exit.

All people consciously or unconsciously set ceilings on how angry they will allow themselves to become before they exit a provocative situation. Even the worst batterers have limits—they may push but not punch or choke but not kill. Hopefully you will set low enough anger ceilings that you will exit in time to do zero damage, verbal or physical, to your spouse.

Emotional expressiveness can be colorful and invigorating. At the same time, staying in a situation beyond the point where you can talk cooperatively is likely to prove both unproductive and hurtful.

Summing Up and Moving On

This chapter has focused on skills for sustaining effective collaborative dialogue. It started with looking at how to braid together your talking and listening so that when you talk together you feel like a close-knit team. You learned to distinguish collaborative from oppositional or parallel dialogue, and how to use friendly interruption. Next you learned how symmetry, short segments, specifics, and summaries can increase your effectiveness when you talk about difficult issues. Lastly this chapter explored a number of heat-control options so that you can keep the emotional climate in your home within a range conducive to sustaining your dialogue skills. When constructive dialogue becomes difficult to sustain because of emotional intensity, a brief pause or an exit from the room can calm you down, so planning for these is important.

Sometimes, alas, challenging circumstances may still provoke upsets. In the coming chapters you will learn more about keeping anger from upsetting your relationship, along with multiple skills for managing difficult conflicts.

CHAPTER 6

Understanding Anger

Of the many emotions that color marriages, anger poses the most challenges. Anger is the quickest emotion to become hurtful and the trickiest to keep helpful.

Anger fires you up to charge ahead with aggressive action, putting you at risk for striking back when thoughtful dialogue or a quick exit might be more helpful.

Can anger be helpful? Absolutely yes. Feelings of irritation let you know where there are minor difficulties that need to be addressed—misunderstandings that need clearing up and systems for the routines of living that need adjusting. Major anger lets you know when serious problems are developing. Anger energizes you so that you do respond. And anger can convey the seriousness of your intentions.

The main principle for keeping anger helpful is to treat anger as a stop sign. What would you do at a stop sign? Pause to gather information. Survey the situation. Then pick an effective route to avert crashes and deliver you, unscathed and without hurting others, to precisely where you want to go.

Build Your Anger Awareness

To respond to your anger as a stop sign you first need to be able to recognize when you are angry. Sound easy? Think of all those difficult times when it was only afterward, upon reflecting back, that you realized how irritated you were. Or recall a time when you thought you were just talking and yet someone asked you, "What are you so mad about?" Think of times you thought you were managing a provocative situation just fine and then suddenly hit overload and blew up.

The more sensitively you can note when you are feeling even the smallest tidbit of anger, the more likely that you will be able to harness your anger effectively.

Recall Your Anger Experiences

Many low-, moderate-, and high-intensity feelings all fall under the term *anger*. To enhance your awareness of the full range of anger feelings referred to in this chapter, recall times when you have felt various flavors of this common feeling.

Read the following list of anger words. Choose ones that you can remember having experienced. Write these in the chart, recalling times when you felt the feeling.

Annoyed	Bothered	Disturbed	Exasperated	Frustrated
Fuming	Hostile	Impatient	Irritated	Miffed
Offended	Raging	Resentful	Upset	Violent

Low Anger Level	
Anger words	*Time you felt this*

Moderate Anger Level	
Anger words	*Time you felt this*

High Anger Level	
Anger words	*Time you felt this*

This anger record gives you access to a library of personal moments that you can refer to as you digest the pages ahead. By reflecting on your past personal experiences, good and bad, with harnessing flare-ups, you can plan most insightfully for how you want to deal with anger in the future.

Talk Together

Families differ enormously in their comfort levels with emotional expressiveness. Discuss the way anger was viewed in the family each of you grew up in. To what extent were these attitudes typical of the community in which your family lived? How did you feel if your parents spoke angrily? In your marriage, what do you want to repeat from each of your parents' ways of dealing with anger? What do you want to choreograph anew?

What Anger Does

Adrenaline and other chemicals surge through your body when you are angry. In addition to producing the feelings we label *anger*, these chemicals produce a series of perceptual shifts and cognitive changes. The role-playing exercise below can give you firsthand experience for observing these shifts and changes within yourself.

Hone Your Skills

Following the four steps in the instructions below, dramatize the role of someone who feels extremely angry. This is your chance to cast aside your normal inhibitions about expressing anger. You may discover venom that you may not even have known you had potential to produce.

After the dramatization, debriefing exercises will help you reflect back on what you experienced. The exercise concludes with a visualization for cleansing your system of any remaining anger toxins generated by the dramatization.

Warnings:

This exercise may be noisy. It requires that you use your most uninhibited dramatic potential. You might want to do it in a room by yourself, when others are not nearby. Do not direct this dramatization at your spouse; aiming such venom toward your spouse is entirely out-of-bounds.

Instructions:

1. Think about a situation in which you felt especially angry at someone other than your spouse.

2. Visualize the person in this situation; notice what the person is doing and saying.

3. Imagine that person now sitting in a chair in front of you.

4. Speaking toward the chair, convey your anger in the strongest, most dramatic way you can.

Checklist:

Which of the following did you experience in your anger dramatization?

_____ I felt increasingly angry.

_____ I felt physically heated and tense.

_____ My thoughts and words about the other person became increasingly negative.

_____ I criticized, blamed, and finger-pointed more than I analyzed the problem.

_____ I began to overgeneralize (he's selfish, she's always mean, I never win, etc.).

_____ I didn't want to hear the other person's point of view.

_____ I was striking back more than I was trying to solve our problem.

If you succeeded in working yourself up to extreme anger in your dramatization, you probably experienced all of the phenomena described above. The more anger you feel, the more intensely you probably experienced anger's physical and mental changes.

Read through the table below, which details the changes anger causes. Put a check mark next to the physical and mental changes you experienced in the dramatization or that you have experienced in real life when you have felt angry.

I Felt This	Body Part	Changes Anger Causes
	Heart	Heart rate speeds up to ready you for aggressive action.
	Hand	Begins finger-pointing. Your finger coordinates with your words, with both pointing at what you didn't like. In extreme anger, your hand may form a fist, making threatening motions as if you were going to hit or punch the person you are angry at.
	Mouth	Sets in firm closure to contain your angry thoughts, or opens spouting venom—toxic harsh, critical, and blaming words.
	Voice	You talk increasingly loud and fast.
	Eyes	See as through dark glasses, viewing the other increasingly negatively. You hyper-focus externally, on the person you are mad at, losing your capacity for insight, for seeing your part in the problem.
	Ears	You become deaf to new information that might contradict your angry beliefs and deaf to the concerns of all but yourself.
	Brain	Turns off, like a computer that freezes. You no longer can take in new information, analyze the problem, or create options for solving the problem. Only your lower brain, in charge of animal-like physical reflexes, keeps functioning, which puts you at risk for physical aggression.

As you become increasingly angry, your senses give you unreliable data, skewed toward the darkly negative. Your darkened readings of the other person mean that you are likely to misinterpret the situation, seeing the other as a significantly worse person than he or she really is and overgeneralizing about how extensive the problem is. "You didn't do the dishes" becomes "You are so lazy!" Your brain ceases to process new information, such as that your spouse was exhausted and fell asleep right after dinner. It gets stuck instead, repeating the same thoughts again and again, such as, "I can't rely on you! You let me down!" Stuck in this way, your brain no longer can think through to an understanding of the problem or to possible solutions.

Before going on to the next topic, take a few minutes to cleanse anger that may remain from the previous exercise.

Decontamination:

1. Close your eyes and picture a positive scene.

2. Include loved ones, and especially your spouse, in the scene you choose.

3. Dwell on three aspects of your spouse that you particularly appreciate.

4. Breathe deeply until you feel confident that all remnants of your dramatized anger have drained away.

Anger, even in role-playing, leaves chemical residues. This visualization exercise neutralizes anger chemicals, replacing them with the biochemistry of love. Use this visualization any time that you want to relax and regain a sanguine perspective.

Anger Hurts You

Irritability, even low level irritability, feeds internal bitterness. Blowing up and attacking in anger will hurt you even more. Angry shouting injures your voice. Exploding anger strains your heart. Physical aggression is as likely to wound you as to wound others.

Angry words, voice tones, and behavior also take an energy toll, exhausting you. Strong anger gives a feeling of power at first, but depletes your energy in the long run. The angrier you become and the longer you remain angry, the more you will feel debilitated afterward. The longer and more intense an anger episode, the longer you are likely to need to recuperate, to regain a normal sense of well-being.

Like vented anger, pent-up anger hurts you. Resentment makes you more vulnerable to illnesses, including cancer. It saps your immune system.

Overall, neither acting in anger nor suppressing anger is likely to serve you well.

Anger Hurts Loved Ones

Meanwhile, anger at your spouse is likely to hurt your spouse. Your negative words and tone of voice convey the implicit toxic message, "You are not okay." Anger conveys disapproval.

How does anger pollute a relationship? By hurting your spouse's feelings, your anger erodes your spouse's stockpile of affection, goodwill, and desire to please you. Furthermore, as much as smiles attract, anger repels. Anger makes you look ugly, unappealing, and less lovable. At the same time, anger corrodes your relationship because the unilateral solutions to problems you impose with your anger will incur resentment.

Angry insistence, for instance, that your dinner hour be shifted from six to seven, may get you a later eating time but at a high cost. You spouse would be likely to feel resentment toward you each dinnertime for many days after.

Bystanders who witness your rage will feel themselves become angry. They will feel angry at your anger and will probably emerge with negative feelings toward you. No one likes someone who spreads bad feeling in the world.

Anger especially upsets children. Anger frightens them. Since childhood thinking is egocentric, young children typically think that they must be the cause of the anger around them, adding feelings of guilt to being scared, angry by contagion, and upset.

Saddest of all, the emotional overstimulation a child experiences when watching or receiving adults' anger can permanently change the child's emotional response system, potentially causing permanent emotional overreactivity. Trauma-induced overreactivity results in a tendency to react to small slights or problems as if they were major insults. This biochemical effect of witnessing or receiving intense anger in childhood may explain why children of angry parents tend to experience anger problems themselves throughout their lives.

All in all, expressions of even low levels of anger tend to be unpleasant, depressing, and corrosive to you, your spouse, your marriage, and your children. High-intensity anger is all the more damaging. Like rust on a car, anger eats away at the happiness of all family members.

The following story by an anonymous author was offered to the writers of this book by a man who has worked hard to tame his quick temper. He hopes the story will help others as it helped him.

An Anger Parable

There once was a little boy who had a bad temper.

His father gave him a bag of nails and told him that every time he lost his temper, he must hammer a nail into the back of the fence.

The first day the boy drove thirty-seven nails into the fence.

Over the next few weeks, as he learned to control his anger, the number of nails hammered daily gradually dwindled down. He discovered it was easier to hold his temper than to drive those nails into the fence.

Finally the day came when the boy didn't lose his temper at all.

He told his father about it. His father suggested that the boy now pull out one nail for each day that he was able to hold his temper.

The days passed. Eventually the young boy was able to tell his father that all the nails were gone.

The father took his son by the hand. He led him to the fence and said, "You have done well, my son, but look at the holes in the fence. The fence will never be the same."

When you say things in anger, they leave a scar just like these holes. You can put a knife in a man and draw it out. It won't matter how many times you say "I'm sorry." The wound is still there.

As this parable so poignantly clarifies, angry words and actions can leave long-lasting wounds. How can angry feelings therefore ever be helpful? Remember that anger is a sign that tells you to stop and pay attention to a problem situation. Yet, as the next exercise illustrates, when anger surges up, stopping to think about how to address the provocative situation effectively can prove challenging.

Four Anger Myths

What sometimes drives you to feel you simply must continue to express your displeasure? Often one or more of the following mistaken beliefs convinces angry people to ram ahead.

Myth #1: I have to get my anger out.

Reality: Psychologists used to think that you had to pour out your anger in order to stop steaming. In fact, the more that you express angry words and dramatize aggressive behavior, the more—not less—angry you will feel.

Anger is like water in a teapot. You need to take it off the burner to stop the steaming. Removing yourself from an anger-inducing situation is effective; pouring out rage is not.

Another reason why people sometimes believe that anger needs to be expressed is that anger can produce an almost sexual sense of momentum, an urge to go all the way. Anger creates the feeling that you simply must keep going with ever-increasing intensity until you experience the anger's full release in an orgasm-like rage.

Unlike sex, however, anger is neither life-enhancing or procreative. Acting angrily accomplishes nothing positive. To the contrary, as discussed above, angry words and actions prove mainly hurtful, with potential to harm you, your spouse, your relationship, and children.

Myth #2: My anger is your fault.

Reality: Have you ever said, "You made me so angry!" These words indicate a belief that when you feel mad, you have no options other than to act in an angry manner. Not so. Pausing and maybe even removing yourself from angry situations to calm down enough to think almost always prove more effective than lashing out.

This belief also implies that you yourself have nothing to do with your anger. In fact, as you learned with regard to climate controls, when someone feels angry, most often the anger stems as much from being tired, hungry, rushed, or overwhelmed as from what another person has done.

Myth #3: Victimhood legitimizes wrongdoing.

Reality: The mistaken belief, "I'm a victim, so I have the right to be angry," can lead you to lose your moral compass. Anger gives you a sense of power, which can puff you up with a false sense of self-righteousness. Power plus false self-righteousness can be a dangerous combination.

If you genuinely are a victim, it is important to figure out how to change the situation and to bring your victimization to an end. Empowered action, addressing the problem effectively, is vital. Feeling like a victim, however, gives you no right to victimize others in return.

Myth #4: My anger means that what I want is holy and what you want doesn't count.

Reality: As angry feelings well up inside of you, you are likely to experience an inflated sense of the importance of what you want. You are likely to become deaf to the concerns of the person toward whom you feel the anger. Beware. Anger can result in your forgetting that there are two of you, and that both of you have legitimate concerns.

Hone Your Skills

The following scenarios show Ellen responding in four different ways to an upsetting situation with her husband Bill. Label the anger myth that feeds each of her responses.

As you do the exercise, notice if some of Ellen's reactions sound especially familiar. Which might you have said?

Ellen and Bill had decided to paint the living room. Ellen picked out a bright white for the walls and a slightly darker tan for the accent trim. Just when they were about to start painting, Ellen's office called with an emergency she had to take care of. Bill offered to take over the painting project and do as much as he could on his own. Ellen thanked him and left for downtown.

When Ellen returned, Bill was almost finished. The walls, however, were not bright white. Bill had decided to paint the walls instead with the tan trim color. Ellen was furious.

Ellen: I'm furious that you switched the colors without checking with me! You shouldn't have changed them without touching base.

Bill: Let's talk this through, Ellen . . .

Ellen: No! I wouldn't be furious if you'd done what we'd agreed. I'm only mad because you tricked me!

Which myth was this? _____

Ellen: I'm furious! I leave for a few minutes and you change the whole idea of the painting on me. How could you do this to me?

Bill: Let's talk this through, Ellen . . .

Ellen: Why? I'm the one who got hurt here. I'm the one who works at home three days a week and has to live with the colors. I can't believe you would do this to me. I have every right to be mad!

Which myth was this? _____

Ellen: I'm furious that you changed the color scheme without checking with me! You shouldn't have changed it without touching base.

Bill: I'm sorry Ellen. I didn't mean to offend you. I was concerned about the walls looking too bright, like marshmallows. I didn't know you felt so strongly about the white.

Ellen: I said I'm angry! I don't care what you thought. I'm mad. I just hate it when you don't listen to me. How many times do I have to tell you I'm mad?

Which myth was this? _____

Ellen: I'm furious that you changed the colors without checking with me!

Bill: Let's talk this through, Ellen . . .

Ellen: Don't interrupt me! I have to get my anger out, and it's not all out yet. You are so inconsiderate! You just go off on your own way! How could you have done this!

Which myth was this? _____

Ellen's four tirades may have been intended to lead to feeling better; in fact they led to further unhappiness all around. As Ellen vented, she worked herself up into even more distress. Meanwhile, by the end of Ellen's tongue-lashings, Bill's pride in his afternoon of painting had evaporated. His desire to participate in any further painting had dissolved into a pool of resentment.

Worse, Ellen never addressed the actual problem situation—the dilemma of the paint color—or found out why Bill had changed the color. Had she stepped back and sought to understand Bill's decision, Ellen might have agreed that the white paint was too bright and that the tan was in fact more attractive on the walls. Maybe Bill would have learned that next time he wanted to change a jointly agreed-upon plan of action, a quick phone call to his wife to touch base before proceeding would be helpful. Or Bill and Ellen both would have realized that they had made the decision to paint without taking time to talk enough about each other's living room décor ideas. Had they talked more about the specifics, Ellen would have explained why she wanted white walls and Bill might have expressed his concerns about too bright a white. Bill then would have known that his wife would not like changing the wall paint to tan, and would have chosen a different course of action. Cheery yellow walls might have delighted them both.

In sum, dealing with difficulties by talking and acting in anger risks hurting you, hurting your spouse, and besmirching your relationship. You are more likely to create further distress than to solve the dilemma that triggered the upset. The next set of exercises details a far more effective strategy.

Anger Is a Stop Sign

To prevent anger from doing harm and to utilize it for positive gains, think of anger not as the green light it may feel like, urging you to press forward, but rather as a stop sign. What do you do at a stop sign? You stop, look, and listen—and then decide how to proceed.

Stop signs are there to give you important information. So is anger. When you feel angry

- *Stop* to calm down.

- *Look* at yourself and the situation.

- *Listen* to at your spouse.

The familiar motto "Stop, look, and listen" can help you remember how to use anger as a stop sign.

Stop, to Calm Down

Stop means literally to stop what you are doing and saying. Stop participating in the situation to which you have been responding with anger. To stop, use the climate controls pause and exit plans you developed in chapter 5.

- Pause in response to mild irritation.

- Exit in response to more provocative situations. Leave well before your anger explodes.

Since anger blocks clear thinking, the initial goal of a pause or a full stop is to calm yourself down. Once you have returned to a normal emotional zone, then you can begin to think about how to deal effectively with the problem. After you both are calmer, you can resume talking together.

What can you do to calm down once you have stopped? Over time you can figure out what works best for you. For now, try taking these steps:

- Breathe. Breathe slowly and deeply, focusing on the air you are inhaling and exhaling.

- Drink water. Drink cool water to cool yourself down. Avoid alcohol.

- Focus elsewhere. Use distraction. Accomplish something that needs doing like laundry or yard work, or enjoy a simple pleasure.

Hone Your Skills

The following questions build on the initial planning for pauses and exits that you did in chapter 5. The more that you detail and rehearse your plans, the more likely you will be to succeed in using them. In the future, any time you feel even the slightest degree of anger, you can take delight in the opportunity to practice your self-calming skills.

What would be a nice chair to for deep breathing? _____

_____

What routine tasks could be calming? _____

_____

What do you enjoy doing that would be a pleasant distraction while your anger subsides?

_____

Right now, practice pausing. Take a deep breath or two. Then get up and drink water.

How do you feel after taking this break? _____

Remember:

- Holding on to your anger brings no prizes.

- Ruminating on what your spouse did or how wronged you feel will not bring improvements in the situation.

- The goal of stopping is to calm yourself.

- As you feel calmer, anger's perceptual and cognitive distortions will ease and you will return to being able to think constructively.

- Putting yourself into a positive emotional state makes you a winner, no matter what the outcome of the conflict.

Look, at Yourself and at the Situation

Once you have taken a brief pause or exited into another room to cool down from a situation that was getting too hot, what would be helpful to look for and think about? When you stop at a stop sign, you look to gather data about potential danger. When you feel anger, you can look about you to understand the problem facing you. Looking when you stop at a stop sign, however, is usually relatively easy. You look left, right, and ahead. With anger, there are five directions to look before you decide how to proceed.

1. Risk factors. Look first at the risk factors you learned about in chapter 5 on climate controls. Ask yourself if you could be hungry, tired, overloaded, rushed, premenstrual, or getting ill.

In addition, think if you might be at risk for intensified anger because of a prior provocative incident. Anger is cumulative. If you are irritated because your spouse is late paying the bills, you will feel this anger more intensely if a few minutes earlier the dog messed the carpet—and even more so if you were frustrated because your spouse insisted that you to be the one to clean it up.

2. Misses. What misunderstandings, mistakes, or misperceptions may be causing problems? Most irritations occur as a result of something you missed—a mistake, a miscommunication, a misunderstanding. If you can find the miss, your anger will be likely to quickly diminish. We will further explore this idea of finding the misses in chapter 10.

3. Your role. What could you have contributed to the difficulty? Focusing on your partner comes naturally when you are angry. By contrast, to the extent that you switch your focus to looking at yourself, to your own part in the problem, you will feel soothed. Paradoxically, the larger the role you discover that you had in the upset, the calmer you will feel.

4. What you want. The hardest question to answer when you feel anger may be, "What do I want?" Anger usually focuses on negatives, on *don't wants*. Identifying instead what you would like to see happen becomes the challenge.

Making matters worse, anger focuses you outward, on the other person—so when you feel angry, you will be tempted to answer, "I want *him* to . . ." or "I want *her* to . . ." Anger focuses you on what you want others to do or change.

Your challenge is to figure out what *you* want to do, not what you want your spouse to do. The trick you learned for *would likes* can help. Answer "What do I want?" by saying, "I want *to* . . ." or "I want *the/a* . . ." Then, rather than "I want him to get in the car," you would say to yourself, "I want to go home." Or, instead of "I want her to put dinner on the table right now," you would realize, "I want a bite of something to eat right away."

5. Action options. What could you do differently that would bring a better result? Now is your chance for creative thinking. The challenge here is to be sure you look for ways to solve the problem that involve actions you yourself can take—not requests that your spouse do this or that.

Sometimes the optimal solution will involve some change from your spouse. In chapter 8 you will learn *fix-it talk* to work with your spouse to create such changes. For now, however, it is good practice to conclude your looking about by asking yourself, "What can *I* do to bring about what I want?"

Hone Your Skills

Curtis and Kim face a series of upsetting moments. Curtis responds by feeling anger, and then quickly remembers to stop. After a few deep breaths, Curtis feels ready to ask himself the five *look* questions.

To fill in the answers to the five *look* questions in Curtis's first dilemma, you can choose from the possible ideas listed below. No need to use all the story ideas. Just pick a potential answer or two for each question.

To help Curtis answer the *look* questions in his second situation, rely on your own imagination to figure out what might have happened.

Curtis tries to take Kim out for a surprise romantic dinner at an expensive restaurant. Just before they order dinner, Kim announces that she wants to go home. Curtis is furious.

Possible story ideas:

- Kim is under pressure to work at home this evening on a project due the next day.

- The restaurant's air-conditioning is blowing directly on her, giving Kim chills; she's worried she'll get ill.

- Checking first whether Kim thought this would be a good night for a dinner out might have been helpful.

- The waiter took a very long time coming to take their order.

- It's almost 8 o'clock and Curtis is starving.

- Curtis wants to rekindle their sexual life, which had been becoming less frequent.

- They could have a romantic evening by their fireplace at home instead.

- The hostess who showed them to their table was rude.

- The restaurant has a carpet that triggered Kim's asthma.

- Kim is feeling suddenly nauseous.

- Kim is exhausted and just wants to go to sleep early.

- Curtis wants to convey to his wife how much he loves her.

- Kim didn't realize the restaurant was meant to be romantic; to her it just looked dark and excessively expensive.

1. What risk factors might be in play? _____

2. What misses might have occurred? _____

_____

_____

3. How may Curtis have contributed to the problem? _____

_____

_____

4. What does Curtis want? _____

_____

5. How could Curtis get what he wants without anger? _____

_____

_____

It drives Curtis crazy to try to watch football games on his little TV. He suggested buying one with a bigger screen, but Kim said a new TV was a silly expenditure. Squinting to find the ball after he has already missed the first quarter, Curtis feels a rush of anger.

1. What risk factors might be in play? _____

2. What misses might have occurred? _____

_____

_____

3. How may Curtis have contributed to the problem? _____

_____

_____

4. What does Curtis want? _____

_____

5. How could Curtis get what he wants without anger? _____

_____

_____

How did you do on inventing answers to the five *look* questions? There are no right or wrong answers. The point is to become increasingly comfortable with thinking through these questions, and to work with them enough that you will remember the five questions when anger arises.

In case you would like to know some possible answers to Curtis's TV anger story, here are a few.

1. **Risk factors:** Curtis is quick to anger because he was already upset at his next-door neighbor. Curtis had just argued with his neighbor because the neighbor's dog's barking keeps Curtis up at night. That would make Curtis exhausted too, another risk factor.

2. **Misses:** Kim and Curtis missed the reality that Curtis needs glasses. Kim had thought that a large TV would cost a lot more than the one Curtis had found to buy secondhand.

3. **Curtis's contribution to the problem:** Curtis had said he wanted a bigger TV so playfully that Kim thought that he was joking. That could be why she had said it sounded silly.

4. **What Curtis wants:** He just wants to see the game.

5. How he could make that happen: He could go to his mom's house, which his mom would love, or to the sports bar down the block.

The point is that when Curtis feels angry, his attention immediately rivets on what he perceives as his spouse's wrongdoing. The five *look* questions help him to gradually switch his focus onto himself and onto the problem situation. Looking inward and outward broadens his view of the dilemma, has a calming effect on Curtis's angry feelings, and leads Curtis to good ideas for solutions.

Interestingly, people with major anger problems—anger that escalates into verbal abuse or physical battering—tend to show extreme difficulties shifting focus the way Curtis did. Batterers lock onto wanting their partner to do this or that. Asking themselves how they contributed to the problem or asking themselves "What do I want?" can feel beyond their reach. Until they can make this cognitive switch, however, they keep repeating coercion, abuse, and raging.

When you feel anger, if your focus remains fixed on your spouse, you put yourself at risk for becoming increasingly angry. Stepping out at an intersection without looking left or right is dangerous. Stepping ahead in angry situations without pausing to look at yourself and at factors in the broader situation is similarly risky.

Listen, to Your Spouse's Side of the Story

Hearing your spouse's point of view can be surprisingly liberating. It can help you to see a provocative situation with an entirely new perspective. The additional information is also likely to lead to better solutions.

To genuinely hear the other side of the story when you have been angry, you may need to remind yourself to use your listening skills. You may need to prompt yourself to listen to learn. Your job is not to point out what is wrong with what your spouse is saying or to judge or criticize. Rather, your task is to listen for what makes sense, for what is useful in what you hear. Expanding your understanding of what happened helps you to move forward.

Hone Your Skills

Returning to the scenarios in the last exercise, construct *how* and *what* questions that would help Curtis to hear Kim's point of view.

At the expensive restaurant Curtis could ask Kim . . .

1. _____

2. _____

Regarding the TV, Curtis could ask Kim . . .

1. _____

2. _____

Talk Together

How has anger affected your problem solving as a couple in the past? What would be the hardest parts for each of you about using the stop, look, and listen response system?

Prevent Wildfires

Anger can spread like a wildfire. One little spark, especially if the tinder is dry, can unleash a wild, uncontrollable fire. How does Smokey prevent wildfires? He understands what starts them and is extra careful when the conditions are ripe. So, too, you can prevent anger.

The next few exercises give you prevention measures for when external conditions make the anger risk high. You will also learn to identify your own inner hot spots, areas of inflammable dry tinder where you need to use extra caution.

Stick to Your Skills

The angrier you or your spouse is feeling, the harder it will be to stick with the basic skills for constructive dialogue. Anger tends to undo all the skills you learned in the first five chapters. It is especially likely to result in the following slippages.

- Anger's tendency to focus you externally, to hyper-focus you on the person you are talking with, can draw you into using crossovers: "You shouldn't have . . . !" "You just want to . . . !" Crossovers are inflammatory.

- Anger can tempt you to use toxic language, deprecating your spouse.

- Anger can tempt you to talk negatively, using *don't want* instead of *would like* language.

- Anger can focus your listening to what's wrong with what you hear, tempting you to answer with *but*.

- Anger can block your hearing so that you learn very little from what the other person is trying to tell you.

With so much potential for backsliding, any time you feel even low-level anger, you are almost always best off pausing, even just by changing the topic for a bit, until you cool down. Be ready to exit if you sense that the situation may prove too flammable.

Hone Your Skills

Tina and Larry sometimes slip back into old habits of angry interchanges. Use the following skills checklist to help you identify the good habits Tina and Larry forget as they overheat.

1. Say it with I-statements.

2. Ask *how* and *what* questions.

3. Use *would like to* statements.

4. Use *when you* statements.

5. Listen to learn (no *but*).

6. Listen for feelings.

7. Focus on the situation, not your spouse.

8. Use tact, not toxicity.

9. Clarify when *we* is *I* or *you*.

10. Avoid *always and never*.

Tina and Larry had agreed to clean all the hair out of the shower drain after each shower. When Larry climbs into the shower, he finds a big wad of hair.

Larry: You always leave hair in the shower. Did you think I wouldn't notice? You're such a slob.

Tina: But you're the one to blame here. Look at this blond hair. It's not mine!

Oops. What are some of the skills Larry and Tina forgot?

1. _____

2. _____

3. _____

This next version sticks to the skills.

Larry: Tina, there's hair in the shower again.

Tina: Oh, gross. I hate finding hair in the shower. What could we each do to help us both remember to clean it out after each shower?

It is Larry's week to clean up the kitchen, and Tina's to cook. When Tina walks into the kitchen she finds dishes drying on the countertops with no room to cook.

Tina: We have to keep the kitchen clean. I don't like that you're so unreliable about your part of the household chores. Did you grow up in a barnyard pigpen?!

Larry: I hate when you accuse me of leaving the kitchen messy. The real disaster zone is your car. It's so gross in there, with week-old lunches. Yuck!

Oops. What are some of the skills Larry and Tina forgot?

1. _____

2. _____

3. _____

Write a version that sticks to the skills.

Tina: _____

_____

Larry: _____

_____

Larry is studying for an important and difficult night school exam. The papers from his desk have spread to a thick layer across the entire floor.

Tina: We'll have to dig our way into this room. Papers are literally flowing off your desk.

Larry: Stop being so picky. Can't you see that I'm really panicked about the exam?

Oops. What skills did Larry and Tina forget?

1. _____

2. _____

3. _____

Write a version that sticks to the skills.

Larry: _____

_____

Tina: _____

_____

Holding on to your communication basics keeps anger from spreading.

Avoid Needless Anger

Many of us habitually respond with irritated voices or angry words to trivial situations in life. Minor irritating situations can almost always be handled more effectively with simple information sharing than with gruff barking.

Most people find that they react with annoyance again and again to the same situations. Repeated arguments about the same situation mean that you and your spouse have not addressed the problem adequately. Repeated arguments mean you have been emoting, not problem solving.

Remember, ranting does not bring forth solutions. It didn't yesterday, and it won't tomorrow. Ranting at best gains short-term compliance—at a significant cost in resentment. Responding to problems by getting mad mainly invites the problems to recur and spreads ill will.

Hone Your Skills

How might you address the following needless angers? Brainstorm several potential solutions to each of these situations. Let those creative juices flow!

Joseph finds himself frustrated every Sunday when he is late to the early service at church because Teri sleeps in and is not ready to leave on time.

Potential solutions:

1. They could go to church separately, with Joseph leaving earlier.

2. _____

3. _____

Laura finds herself angry when she comes home from work on Tim's Daddy Days and dinner is not ready. She wants to be able to eat right away.

Potential solutions:

1. _____

2. _____

3. _____

Julian finds himself furious when he discovers, yet again, gardening tools left outside in the rain. The expensive new clippers are already showing signs of rust.

Potential solutions:

1. _____

2. _____

3. _____

Finding solutions will sometimes be easy and sometimes more challenging. However, even without solutions, anger as a response to routine living dilemmas is far less serviceable than good-humored information sharing and brainstorming.

Talk Together

What situations in your life together give rise to needless angers that repeatedly crop up? If avoiding repeats of needless angers feels difficult, you may be relieved to know that in future chapters you'll be learning conflict resolution skills for handling these kinds of dilemmas.

Avoid "Should"-Induced Anger

Another line of thinking that can easily induce preventable anger is moralistic judging. As we discussed in chapter 5, saying what your spouse *should* do leads to your feeling cheated or insulted.

- "He should have remembered my birthday."

- "She should know better than to talk about my mother when I'm tired!"

Should thinking almost always invites negative feelings.

What can you do when you hear yourself stoking your inner flames with *should* thinking about your spouse? Remember to change *should* to *could* for a good starter technique. That switch alone can change the feeling inside you from pressure to opportunity.

Another method of calming yourself is to give yourself a quick dose of acceptance therapy.

The *should* thought: He should have remembered my birthday.

Acceptance therapy: "Well, that's the way he is. Birthdays just aren't on his radar screen. He might even forget his own birthday. What a character—he forgets my birthday, and then on some random day comes home with a dozen roses."

Adding a dose of *count-your-blessings therapy* is a powerful next step to undoing *should*-induced anger.

Count-your-blessings therapy: "Actually, I'm lucky. I am really good about remembering birthdays. I guess that's a special ability I have that I've just been taking for granted. I am fortunate."

Counting your blessings shifts the focus from resenting your spouse's disability to appreciating your own special ability. Regarding your ability to do what your spouse does not do as a special blessing leaves you feeling good about yourself instead of annoyed at your loved one.

Hone Your Skills

This exercise lets you practice changing *should*-induced anger to acceptance and then to a blessing. The first two examples are changed already to illustrate how to do it. Can you feel the angry fire die down as you translate each *should* to acceptance? And to a sense of thankfulness?

Should-induced anger	Acceptance	Am I blessed!
She should lose weight. She shouldn't get fat!	She's put on pounds. I'd prefer if she could lose some. If she won't, I'll need to get used to it. She still is soft and loving.	Am I lucky that I love sports and workouts, so I don't have a potbelly yet!
He should spend less money!	He loves to buy nice things. I'll suggest we do a talk together, though, before he buys big-ticket items.	I sure am glad that I am naturally conservative in my spending!
He shouldn't have spoken that way to me!		
She should show more appreciation!		
He shouldn't ignore my mom like that!		

Be Cautious near Land mine Issues

Land mines left in former war zones can be difficult and dangerous to clear. Similarly, each of us generally has a few specific sensitive issues—concerns that have emerged from emotionally intense earlier experiences in our lives, maybe from far back in childhood. When these old sensitivities are touched, we easily feel hurt or upset.

Fortunately, you can learn where your and your spouse's land mine issues lie in the mental landscape you each carry with you. To become familiar with them, discuss these issues with particularly gentle tact. Next time you find yourselves near them, you may even be able, carefully, to defuse them.

Hone Your Skills

The following table lists a number of potential land mine issues. Rate on a scale of 1 to 10 how sensitive you are to this concern (1 equals virtually not at all; 10 equals an explosive land mine). Then, think about outbursts in your life that have stemmed from these land mine issues.

Land mine issue	Rate from 1–10	What angry outbursts do you recall that might have stemmed from this land mine?
Feeling taken advantage of		
Feeling unheard, not listened to		
Feeling unloved or unappreciated		
Feeling controlled		
Feeling shamed or humiliated		

Feeling left out		
Feeling unimportant		
Feeling you do more than your share		
Other:		

Mapping your land mines can help you to predict where the territory is likely to be dangerous so that you then can be especially meticulous about your dialogue skills. Slow down, scan ahead, and proceed with careful attention to safe talking and listening.

Create an Anger Profile

Charting the moments when you experience irritation or anger can help you to see patterns in when, where, and why you tend to become angry. Awareness is the first step toward good choices about what you will do in the future. When you recognize that the tinder may be dry, you can be especially cautious not to start a wildfire.

If you experience frequent anger, make copies of this chart, or replicate it in a notebook. Fill in the chart daily until you feel that you have succeeded in significantly ending anger's toxic role in your marriage.

My Anger Profile

Date and time	Kind of anger (irritation, etc.)	Risk factors (tired, hungry, etc.)	What I wanted	What I recall thinking or saying, and what I did

Particularly if you experience irritation or anger with some frequency (once a week or more), reviewing your chart after each several entries will begin to clarify patterns. To help you recognize patterns, try answering the following questions.

At what times of day, and in what kinds of situations, do you experience anger? _____

_____

_____

Over what concerns do you seem to be most likely to become angry? _____

_____

What risk factors may make these times especially difficult for you? _____

_____

_____

Reflect back on your angry incidents. Were any fueled by an anger myth? Which were examples of a needless anger? A *should*-induced anger? A land mine issue? List your angry moments by anger categories. You will probably find that some anger incidents falls into more than one box.

Anger myth? (Note which one)	Needless anger?	*Should*-induced? (Note the *should*)	Land mine issue? (Note which)

Look back once again at the angry moments you recorded. Make a star next to each moment where you were able to stop, look, and listen and stick to your skills instead of allowing the anger to escalate. Hooray if you have some stars there!

Now, circle the date and time of moments that you would have liked to handle differently. For each moment with a circle, reconsider how you would have preferred to handle the situation. If you circled more than two moments, use additional paper to continue this exercise until you have worked through all of them.

1. Situation: _____

Skills I could have used: _____

_____

New response: _____

_____

_____

2. Situation: _____

Skills I could have used: _____

_____

New response: _____

_____

_____

Talk Together

Discuss your Anger Profile with your spouse. Share your answers. What situations did you both write down? What have each of you learned about these moments?

Summing Up and Moving On

The bottom line: Angry feelings help to the extent that they make you aware of a problem that needs to be addressed. Addressing the problem with angry words and actions, however, almost always does more harm than good. Would you pick up a stop sign and clobber people with it? Anger similarly is not for clubbing people. Anger is a stop sign. Stop, look, and listen. Then devise a strategy for proceeding ahead.

In this chapter you have also learned that anger can spread like wildfire. What if you are not angry, but your spouse is? The next chapter looks at skills for situations in which your spouse is getting hot, and you don't want to get burned.

CHAPTER 7

Receiving Anger

The receiving end of anger is unpleasant. Whereas feeling anger brings energizing self-righteous indignation and a puffed-up sense of power, anger directed at you is designed to induce the opposite feelings. You are likely to feel tarnished or diminished, resentful, hurt, or even frightened by the attack. In response, you become at risk for flipping into anger as well, puffing up for a defensive counterattack.

Are feeling bad or fighting back your only options? Fortunately, no. You have a myriad of possibilities when you receive an irritated voice or an angry comment. For instance, you could

- answer matter-of-factly

- respond in a soothing way

- reply with tension-relieving humor or affection

- offer helpful additional information

- think to yourself about what could be troubling the person who is exploding

- take a quick cool-down pause

- step out of the room to a safety zone

The goal of receiving anger is to transform the attack into an opportunity for understanding and solving a problem. Collapsing emotionally into hurt feelings or flaring back in anger signals that you have slipped from problem-solving about the dilemma into defeat, attacking, or defending.

This chapter details a number of techniques for transforming angry attacks into constructive collaborative dialogue. At the same time, when you are in doubt, find a way out. If you feel uncertain about whether or not you can handle your spouse's anger without feeling burned or flaring up yourself, use your pause or exit.

You will notice one difference in this chapter from the rest of the book. Elsewhere, we give examples of many different couples using the skills you are learning. We intend to convey that all kinds of couples can learn to benefit from these skills. In this chapter, all of the examples and exercises involve one couple, Van and Flora. Van and Flora often make the mistake of directing angry comments at each other. The hurtful interchanges you read in this chapter between Van and Flora are not ones to emulate.

Respond Constructively or Exit

In every marriage partnership, a comment, tone of voice, or action sometimes touches a sensitive nerve. One error alone, however, does not make a fight. Arguing only ensues if the receiver replies back in a negative, defensive, or counterattacking way.

Sometimes one spouse picks a fight, seemingly looking for an excuse to express anger, criticize, or pound on someone. In these cases, which are common in abusive situations, arguments may not be so mutual. One person alone pretty much initiates the negativity. Often these cases, nothing the receiver of the anger does, short of exiting from the situation, is likely to stop escalation.

Most of the time, however, particularly in garden-variety household squabbles, arguments erupt because one of the participants became hot under the collar. The receiver of anger, in these cases, has a key position. When you hear anger in your spouse's tone of voice, how you respond can make all the difference between mutual escalation and a return to cooperation.

Agree, Don't Argue

"If you can't fight them, join them." Finding something to agree with is a potent way to diffuse anger. Agreeing in some way with your spouse's angry comment will help to put you both on the same side, returning you to feeling more like partners instead of adversaries.

Agreeing means using the basic listening skills you learned in chapter 3. Listen carefully for what makes sense about what your spouse is saying. Find an aspect you can say yes to. Then digest aloud what you heard, detailing what you agree with in your spouse's comment:

- "Yes (giving specifics which you agree with), and . . ."

- "I agree that . . ."

- "I appreciate that . . ."

- "I can see that . . ."

After you have established an element that you agree about, you are more likely to be able to add your views and have them received without continued hostility. *Yes, and* responses, by signaling agreement, invite agreement in return.

Hone Your Skills

Van and Flora are both often on the receiving end of angry comments. Help them to find something to agree with in response. Create calm *yes, and* responses that detail agreement before adding further information.

Flora: The rug looks like it hasn't been vacuumed in a month! It makes us look like total slobs.

Van: *Yes,* I agree that the rug does look terrible, *and* I think it's from the dog tracking in mud yesterday after that rainstorm.

1. *Van:* You left the milk out on the kitchen counter again!

Flora: Yes _____

   and, _____

   _____

2. *Flora:* You were zipping all over and flirting at that party. You totally ignored me!

Van: Yes _____

   and, _____

   _____

3. *Van:* You woke me up again. I hate it when you do that; I can never get back to sleep.

Flora: Yes _____

   and, _____

   _____

Why does agreement calm anger? First, the initial words of a conversation make a bid in the ever-present unspoken bargaining for dialogue mode. If your spouse has put forth a bid for adversarial dialogue, you can still make a counteroffer. Your counterbid for calm talking may win.

At the same time, angry people generally push hard because they believe that otherwise what they want to say will not be heard. When you agree, you are showing that your listening is open and receptive. Your spouse can relax, no longer feeling a need to barge through. Both of you then can proceed more calmly.

Detoxify

As you have learned before, responding to toxic harsh comments without getting defensive can be tricky. You can learn, however, to let toxicity roll off like water on Teflon. To respond calmly and also take in the useful information your spouse is trying to convey, use detoxification.

Detoxification starts with agreeing. Agree with *yes, and,* as you were practicing above. When you come to pejorative words or phrases, however, translate the toxic into tactful words:

1. Respond with *yes.* Find something you can agree with.

2. As you digest aloud what makes sense to you, translate the toxic words into milder tactful words.

3. Add your own point of view.

In the following example, for instance, Van responds with a *yes, and.* In the midst of it, he translates the harsh word *lunatic* into "driving too fast without realizing it."

Van is driving aggressively to get to a meeting and almost gets into an accident. Flora, frightened, bursts out, "Lunatic!"

Detoxified   Yes. You're right. I was driving too fast without even realizing it. And
response: fast driving isn't worth the risk. I'll slow down.

Hone Your Skills

Practice detoxifying as you help Van and Flora to handle the following verbal attacks. Circle the toxic word or words in each angry statement. Then, in your *yes, and* response substitute a more neutral word or phrase for the toxic ones that you have circled. Note: An effective *yes, and* response can have either the *yes,* or the *and* implied as in the example we have completed. Just be sure there is no *but* or *however.*

Van just spilled a cup of coffee on Flora's pants as they were about to dash off to work. Flora, in panicked annoyance, shouted, "Your stupid coffee addiction is making me late for work."

Van's   Oops. You're right. That cup of coffee made a pretty visible stain on your
detoxified   pants, and we sure are running late. I think part of the reason everything
response: feels so rushed is that the alarm wasn't set early enough.

Before going to the movies Flora mentioned what a friend had told her about the movie's theme. Van snapped, "Your blabbing motormouth has ruined the film for me. I hate hearing about movies before I see them."

Flora's
detoxified   _____
response: _____

Flora and Van went clothes shopping together. When Flora asked for feedback about the sixth black dress she was trying, Van blurted, "You look ugly in that dress."

Flora's
detoxified _____
response: _____

Van was grilling in the backyard when the phone rang. By the time he returned to the grill, a burger had caught on fire. Flora, seeing the flames yelled, "You nutcase! What were you thinking leaving the grill going like that?"

Van's
detoxified _____
response: _____

Name-calling and other toxic ways of describing each other do not belong in husband-wife dialogue. They sometimes occur, which is why it is important to have detoxification response skills. It helps to be prepared for difficult moments. At the same time, remember that toxic comments are out-of-bounds in healthy couple dialogue.

Toxic voice tones also are out-of-bounds. As the saying goes, the melody makes the music. Fortunately, detoxification can work with tone of voice as well as with words. When your spouse speaks to you in an irritated voice, responding in a normal cooperative tone hopefully will convert the dialogue back from fighting to friendly.

Receiving an occasional toxic comment or hearing a rare irritated voice is part of accepting that your spouse is human. Receiving an ongoing diet of critical words or irritated tones is another matter altogether. A household with frequent anger, including even low-level irritation, is at best needlessly unpleasant. At worst, receiving too much anger can leave you feeling verbally abused.

If you often need to detoxify, or if the anger that drives the toxic comments feels more frequent or intense than you want in your day-to-day life space, then it's time to *say it*. Raise your concerns about hurtful language and tone of voice with your spouse. Come to agreement about the extent to which either of you are going to speak hurtfully in the future and plan how to accomplish the change.

Return to Your Listening and Talking Skills

Agreeing uses the basic listening skills you learned earlier. Agreeing means that you listen to learn, give evidence of what you have taken in by digesting aloud, and respond with *and* rather than *but*. Similarly, all of your basic talking guidelines can help you to convert anger directed your way back to cooperative dialogue.

Remember the basic rule that prevents crossovers. Any time you speak you can *talk about yourself or ask about the other person*. Say your thoughts and feelings with I-statements. Ask *how* and *what* questions.

As long as you give readouts of your thoughts and feelings using I-messages, you will be unlikely to slip into crossovers. Avoiding you-statements, which tend to be inflammatory in any situation, is all the more important when your spouse already is irritated. As we discussed earlier, if the anger pump is already primed with prior anger, additional irritants will have a stronger impact.

Asking *how* and *what* questions can be especially fruitful. Good questions can give an irritated spouse an impetus to shift from emoting to analyzing. Good questions can assist an irritated spouse with identifying and understanding the problem. If your spouse is too angry or fixed in blame to be able to respond in a thinking mode, however, persisting with questions can prove antagonizing instead of helpful, so use your judgment.

Hone Your Skills

Label the talking and listening skills that Flora demonstrates as she responds successfully to Van's irritation. This list of skills is the same as the one you used in chapter 6 for when you yourself feel angry. Any time that either you or your spouse feel anger, both of you will benefit from holding a tight rein on your skills.

1. Say it with I-statements.

2. Ask *how* and *what* questions.

3. Use *would like to* statements.

4. Use *when you* statements.

5. Listen to learn (no *but*).

6. Listen for feelings.

7. Focus on the situation, not your spouse.

8. Use tact, not toxicity.

9. Clarify when *we* is *I* or *you*.

10. Avoid *always* and *never*.

Van: (irritated) Why in heaven's name are you taking so many suitcases!

Flora: Yes, I am taking two quite large suitcases. The plane lets us take two,   _____
and I have a lot of gifts for my family.

Van: We shouldn't take so much. You are packed like a camel.

Flora: Yes, I also prefer to travel light, and I couldn't figure out how to do   _____
that and bring at least something for everyone. I do have a big family.

Van: You're going overboard.

Flora: I'm concerned about how negative you sound. What's going on?   _____
What about my suitcases bothers you? When you sound this grumpy,
I figure something's worrying you.

Van: I look at the suitcases—I see back trouble. I always get a backache from
carrying suitcases.

Flora: I do recall you often have had back problems after lugging my bags. _____
   This trip I'm glad to handle my suitcases myself. They both have
   wheels. A baggage handler showed me how to lift them by bumping
   them up with my knee. I can handle them without help easily now.

As Van and Flora's suitcase dialogue illustrates, using your communication guidelines when your spouse is annoyed can lead back to calm. Still, bear in mind the limits of the power of healthy communication to return an angry dialogue onto a positive track. Only withdrawing can bring safety from some rising anger tides.

Review Your Pause and Your Exit and Reentry Routines

The backup plan for disengaging on the receiving end of anger is the same as the routine for when you feel yourself heating up. *Stop* with a pause, or take an exit to remove yourself from situations you may not be able to handle cooperatively. Then *look*, and *listen*. Look at your risk factors, your misses, your role in the problem, what you want and your action options. Listen to your spouse's concerns.

Remember, if one of you is at all irritated or angry, odds are high that soon neither of you will be able to talk effectively about the troubling situation.

If the two of you have come to an agreement that you both want to control the emotional climate in your home by ceasing any conversation that raises harsh or irritated voices, you are likely to succeed. If your basic talking and listening skills don't calm matters quickly, exit the conversation. It's better to be safe than sorry.

Return to Problem-Solving

Remember what anger is good for. Like a stop sign, anger indicates the presence of a problem.

If your response to an angry comment is calm, good-humored, and collaborative, your spouse may be able to join you in a return to productive dialogue. Productive dialogue identifies the problem and leads to solutions.

Focus on the Problem

Focusing on the problem, instead of on your spouse or on his or her angry comment, helps to block the impulse to return a hostile volley. As with agreeing, focusing on the problem invites constructive talking.

In the following example, Van forgets to focus on the situation. He inflames an already hot situation by responding to Flora's pique with negative comments about her and her anger.

Van has cut in front of Flora in the buffet line.

Flora: How rude!

Van: Stop snapping at me! Who are you, Mrs. Perfect, that you can criticize me?

If Van had remembered to focus on the problem situation rather than on his spouse, he could have calmed the situation instead of inflaming it further.

Flora: How rude!

Van: Oops. I'm starving. All I was thinking about was getting to that food. Would you mind if I join you? Meanwhile, I'm going to grab a nibble of that stuffed mushroom!

Hone Your Skills

Hopefully your spouse does not blurt out unpleasant comments like Van and Flora sometimes do. However, in case an occasional toxic comment does slip out, be ready to steer clear of reciprocal responses. Defuse the anger by refocusing on the situation.

Practice in the following examples by helping Van and Flora identify the problem.

Van is angry that Flora leafed through papers on his desk. "Your snooping has wrecked my system for knowing what's where!" he snaps. Flora, who had been looking for their plane tickets, retorts, "Jeepers, you're so suspicious. You get mad at nothing!"

Flora would have been more helpful if she had focused on the problem, saying: _____

_____

_____

Flora is annoyed because laundry is Van's job and the laundry hasn't been done for ten days. When she complains in a tone of clear annoyance, Van snaps back, "You never put your clothes in the hamper. It's your fault the laundry's not done. There's not enough clothes in the hamper to even think about starting a load. You should be mad at yourself, not me."

Van would have been more helpful if he had focused on the problem, saying: _____

_____

_____

Van is upset that Flora hasn't yet worn the fancy lingerie he bought her. Flora reacts by focusing on him, "Leave me alone! You're so controlling! I'll wear what I please when I please."

Flora would have been more helpful if she had focused on the problem, saying: _____

_____

_____

Focusing on the problem helps Van and Flora to identify what about the situation raised their ire. Instead of blaming and escalating, by focusing on the problem, they set the stage for productive problem solving. In the desk example above, for instance, Flora might have responded, "I did go through the papers. I wanted to check when we arrive in L.A. so I could arrange for a ride from the airport. What if we put joint papers like plane tickets in a special bos."

In the laundry example, instead of a blaming retort, Van could have kept his focus on the problem by analyzing the situation. "I think I get stymied when you leave your dirty clothes on a chair instead of in the hamper. I've been watching the hamper to know when I need to do a wash load. Maybe I could set a standard laundry time each week, like every Sunday night, rather than going by the hamper. Then you'd know when I'm going to wash and could be sure you've given me your dirty clothes. How would that work for you?"

As to the lingerie situation, how would the dialogue have proceeded if Flora had answered, "I can't remember where I put the new things. They're so pretty. I hate to admit that I can't recall where I put them. Or that when I find them I'm still going to be a bit shy about wearing them. Pretty risqué for me—."

Your answers to the questions above may have invented totally different circumstances. The point is that as long as their focus is on the problem, not on their spouse's anger, Van and Flora's responses would be helpful.

Master "It's Not about Me"

Taking your spouse's anger personally can distract you from focusing on the problem. Taking it personally, or as therapists say, *personalizing* your spouse's anger, is easy to do if the anger is expressed as toxic comments about you.

Van: How could you have scratched this CD? You know I like this band so much! How could you have ruined something I love like this?

Flora: How can you speak that way to me? Do you think I'm just a rug to stomp on? You must not respect me.

As in the example above, your angry spouse's comments may in fact focus on you instead of on the problem. If you take the personalizing route, however—"How dare he say that to me! What does he think I am!"—you will be likely to strike back in hurt and anger. Instead, try to interpret your spouse's anger as a sign that something specific is troubling him or her rather than as a sign of how he or she really regards you.

Van: How could you have broken this CD I like so much!?

Flora: (*thinking to herself*) I wonder why he's getting so upset about a broken CD? Accidents happen, and usually he adapts easily. Why is this one so upsetting for him? Is it because he's so stressed by work? Overtired? Worrying about money? Worrying about being able to find another copy, in case the stores don't carry that one anymore? I'd better ask questions, so we can figure out together what's going on.

Hone Your Skills

Since the more angry people feel, the more negatively they view the other person, the you-statements your spouse issues in anger have potential to sound quite threatening if you take them to heart.

Van and Flora have been working hard to reduce their arguing. In the following dialogues, the sense of threat diminishes when Van and Flora remind themselves "It's not about me," and instead focus on identifying the problem that troubles their spouse. Using the first example as a model, try filling in Van and Flora's responses in the remaining dialogues.

1. Flora: You put another dent in the car!

Van: *(making her anger about him)* You think I'm incompetent. I can't help it if someone opened a car door into the side of our car in the parking lot.

Alternatively, Van reminds himself "It's not about me" and finds out Flora's concerns.

2. Van: Are you upset because another body shop bill won't fit in our budget? That's what disturbs me. What about you?

Van: Don't tell me you burned the bottom of another pot!

Flora: *(making his anger about her)* If you're telling me I'm a hopeless cook, you can cook for yourself!

Alternatively, Flora reminds herself "It's not about me" and finds out Van's concerns:

Flora: _____

_____

3. Flora: You threw out the magazine I was reading! I left it open purposely so you would know I wasn't finished.

Van: *(making her anger about him)* You think I'm out to get you all the time. How much does a guy have to take!

Alternatively, Van reminds himself "It's not about me" and finds out Flora's concerns:

Van: _____

_____

Taking anger personally can lead you to feel upset, depressed, guilty, or filled with righteous indignation. If, by contrast, you calmly focus on the problem triggering your spouse's anger, you can help both you and your spouse handle the situation in a more productive manner.

Ask About Concerns

Guessing or assuming you know the upsetting dimension of a problem may be tempting. Asking will give you more accurate information. You may be surprised how often you misidentify the disturbing part. Ask what they are.

Hone Your Skills

In response to the following situations, create questions that would help Van and Flora identify the problem that needs solving. *How* and *what* will be your best starter words.

Van snaps at Flora because she left the garage door unlocked while she took their toddler around the block on her tricycle.

Flora: What are you worried might happen if the door is open a few minutes?

Flora starts complaining about how often Van's parents visit.

Van: _____

_____

Van just bought a new piano, and now Flora is muttering in annoyance.

Van: _____

_____

Everyone likes to feel that their spouse cares when they feel distressed. Asking questions that seek to understand your spouse is likely to yield a positive response.

Still, anger's cognitive distortions sometimes doom attempts to invite an angry spouse to return to constructive problem solving. Remember, the more anger, the more likely the brain will shut down, ears close, eyes see darkly, and fingers point. Consequently, attempts to talk cooperatively with a spouse who feels adversarial often may not succeed. If the anger continues, be sure to exit.

Talk Together

Attempting to talk over concerns while one of you is angry may or may not work for the two of you? Have there been times when it has backfired? How has the anger's duration or intensity affected your ability as a couple to talk effectively once one of you has begun heating up?

Practice with Your Partner

Learning to put the anger-response skills you have learned into use in real conversations will take time and practice. The following drill will allow you to practice these skills with your partner in a controlled environment.

Read the following angry comments. As one of you reads the angry sentence, the other responds using the skills from this chapter. Check the box next to each skill that your response accomplishes.

Switch who reads the angry sentence when you start the next example.

1. "I asked you not to put glasses on the end table! You shouldn't be so careless! Look at the ring it left!"

   ____ Agree

   ____ Detoxify

   ____ Focus on the problem

   ____ Avoid personalizing; remember, "It's not about me."

   ____ Ask about concerns

2. "You were supposed to call to get the phone hooked up. You're so spacey."

_____ Agree

_____ Detoxify

_____ Focus on the problem

_____ Avoid personalizing; remember, "It's not about me."

_____ Ask about concerns

3. "Can't you see I'm busy! Don't be such a nagging ninny. Just let me be."

_____ Agree

_____ Detoxify

_____ Focus on the problem

_____ Avoid personalizing; remember, "It's not about me."

_____ Ask about concerns

4. "You did what? You took the baby walking in this frigid weather! That was really dumb!"

_____ Agree

_____ Detoxify

_____ Focus on the problem

_____ Avoid personalizing; remember, "It's not about me."

_____ Ask about concerns

All of the angry statements above violate the guidelines for constructive dialogue. However, these you-statements and toxic words typify the unfortunate comments spouses can make when anger clouds their judgment. Could you feel in this exercise how your power increases as you learn to stay calm and bring about more productive dialogue?

While skills at receiving anger without getting hurt or mad can serve you well, it is important to know at the same time that you are not responsible for calming your spouse's anger. Each of you is responsible for managing your own emotional states. If you can help your spouse to dampen occasional moments of fire, fine. On the whole, however, whereas children depend on adults to soothe them, adults monitor and maintain their own emotional equilibrium. Marriage is for adults.

While you are not responsible for keeping your spouse calm, you are responsible for maintaining your emotional safety. If your spouse, for whatever reason, locks into an angry stance, your responsibility is to exit. If your spouse locks into frequent and destructive episodes of anger, get help.

Summing Up and Moving On

In this chapter you have learned several skills for receiving anger.

- Before responding to any angry comment, make sure that you are calm enough to respond in a way that will be constructive, not aggressive.

- Agree, detoxify, and move forward.

- Focus on the practical issues that need to be solved. Ask about concerns.

- If agreeing and attempts at problem solving do not result in soothing and resumed cooperation, exit. Wait a bit and try again.

The next chapter covers some new skills that will help you prevent angry blowups from occurring in your marriage.

CHAPTER 8

Dealing with Differences

Ah, the power of two to invite conflict. Conflicts—those moments in which you want one thing and your spouse seems to want another—arise because in marriage there are two of you. If marriage involved just you alone, how easy it would be to have no fighting! Alas, with two, life is more complex. You live together in shared spaces. You share finances. You have innumerable decisions to make together, each one a potential point of conflict.

The good news is that you can develop win-win skills that will help you resolve virtually any and every marriage conflict. Without these skills, conflicts tend to lead to fights or, to avoid fights, silences. With these skills, conflicts trigger information sharing and conclude with a plan of action that pleases you both.

As you will see in the coming pages, successful conflict resolution requires all the skills you have learned thus far for talking and listening cooperatively. Adversarial stances have no place here. Anger needs to be cooled. Bilateral listening with each of you looking out for the other's best interests as well as for your own enables talking toward solutions.

This chapter begins with the three basic steps of what we call the *win-win waltz*. It then gives you practice using this strategy as you make decisions together and resolve conflicts.

The Three Steps of the Win-Win Waltz

The win-win waltz can consistently lead you from conflicting ideas to a shared perspective. With practice, this strategy for moving from conflict to agreement flows smoothly. Like a waltz, the process relies on three steps:

Step 1: Express initial positions.

- Say what you would like.

- Listen to what your spouse would prefer.

Step 2: Explore underlying concerns.

- Identify the factors, preferences, hopes, fears, desires, or other concerns to which your initial position is a response.

- Add those of your spouse, putting the concerns of you both on one list.

Step 3: Generate solution options.

- Create a plan of action that responds to all the concerns of both of you.

- Last question: Are there any final pieces that still feel unfinished?

The win-win waltz worksheet that follows lays out these steps visually. There are three boxes, one for each of the steps. You will be using the worksheet in upcoming exercises, but take a look at the blank worksheet.

Notice that the first box, the box for step one, is split into two sides. One side is for your positions or preferences, and the other for your partner's. "Let's have soup for supper." "No, let's have spaghetti." It's normal, when you launch shared decision-making, for you to feel somewhat at odds, each proposing a different plan of action. The two separate sides reflect this sense of split.

The second and third boxes, by contrast, each have just one shared list. The single list indicates that by step two, you are working together as partners. "I'm concerned about getting rid of these sniffles, so I thought chicken soup would help." "And I'm just real hungry, after running such a long distance today. That's why I'm craving something substantial like pasta." Any concern of one of you immediately becomes a concern of both, so both concerns get added to the one partnership list.

The main magic of the win-win waltz occurs in this transition from step one, feeling like separate players espousing seemingly contradictory plans, to step two. Suddenly you become collaborative partners. That switch happens because action plans, soup or spaghetti, the stuff of step one, may be mutually contradictory—we can either do your way or mine. Concerns, the content of step two, by contrast, almost always can dovetail.

In step three, similarly, the box is undivided; you are working collaboratively. Any solution one of you proposes needs to be designed to work equally well for you both. Both of your concerns count as you look for a responsive plan of action. "How about if first I give you one of my potent wellness vitamin pills. Then let's have chicken soup, with a ton of noodles. I'll eat lots, and you can add just what noodles you want to your bowl. Let's defrost a loaf of bread from the freezer too, for even more carbs." This solution, responding to the underlying concerns on both sides, proves not only mutually acceptable, but even better than either spouse's original suggestion. When both of you look out for both of your interests, that's marriage partnership at its best.

The Win-Win Waltz Worksheet

Step 1: Express initial positions	
Yours: "I'd like to . . ."	Your spouse's: "I'd like to . . ."

Step 2: Explore underlying concerns
•
•
•
•
•

Step 3: Generate solution options
Your initial solution, with modifications to include spouse's concerns:
Spouse's initial solution, with modifications to include your concerns:
New ideas altogether:
Our plan is:
Are there any little pieces of this that still feel unfinished?

Laurie and Tory filled in the completed sample worksheet below to change an initial disagreement into a mutually acceptable plan. They are using the worksheet to decide how to unpack in their new apartment.

Sample Win-Win Waltz Worksheet

Laurie and Tory are moving into a new apartment. They are trying to figure out where to start unpacking.

Step 1: Express initial positions	
Laurie's: "I'd like to ..."	Tory's: "I'd like to ..."
start by unpacking boxes in the kitchen together.	*start by working together to get my office set up.*

Step 2: Explore underlying concerns
• *We'll both become irritable if we don't eat.*
• *There's only eight hours left for unpacking, and fully unpacking will probably take way more time.*
• *Tory needs his home office for work tomorrow.*
• *Laurie wants unpacking to be fun together time.*
• *Laurie needs help lifting things because of a bad back.*

Step 3: Generate solution options
Your initial solution, with modifications to include spouse's concerns: *Get takeout food instead of unpacking the kitchen. Focus together on office unpacking.*
Spouse's initial solution, with modifications to include your concerns: *Clear off the kitchen table then focus on unpacking the office.*
New ideas altogether: *Play music. Call for take-out food.*
Our plan is: *I'll try phoning for the takeout food and see if they'll deliver while you clear the kitchen table. Then we can start unpacking the office together right away, starting with the box of CD's.*
Are there any little pieces of this that still feel unfinished?   *Where is the boom box?*

In the sample worksheet, Laurie and Tory used the win-win waltz steps to change initial disagreement into a mutually acceptable plan. Here's how the dialogue outlined in the sample worksheet sounded. Notice how, even though Laurie and Tory began with a conflict, the three steps flow smoothly in an atmosphere of good-humored cooperation.

Step 1: Express initial positions.

Laurie: What a mess. This could be overwhelming. I'd like to start with the kitchen.

Tory: Gosh, I'd much rather start with the office.

Laurie and Tory's visions differ for where to start unpacking their stacks of boxes. Laurie acknowledges these differences and moves to the second win-win waltz step.

Step 2. Explore underlying concerns.

Laurie: Looks like we have different ideas about where to start. I vote the kitchen, so I can cook. Without being able to refuel, I'll never make it through this mountain of boxes without getting pissy. I'm verging on panic as it is, with what looks like two days at least of work and just one day to do it. Being hungry won't help.

Tory: I totally agree that it's important that we eat well while we're unpacking. If we don't, we'll both get cranky. I'd like to start with the office, though. Otherwise we might not get the computers hooked up in time for me to work on Monday.

Laurie: We could each do separate rooms; at the same time, I'd prefer to work together. We get so little time together with the travel I have to do for my job. I like being able to have a full day with you in the same room. Besides, it will be more fun, especially if we put on upbeat music.

Tory: And if we work in the same room, I can help you more easily with heavy boxes. That back of yours isn't fully healed. If I'm in a different room, I'll be worrying you're not asking for help with lifting.

Having delineated their concerns, Tory and Laurie move forward to step three, brainstorming on solution options. Notice how responsive they are to each other's concerns—without giving up on their own. They exemplify bilateral listening.

They also successfully avoid focusing crossover-style on what they want the other to do. Instead, they each take personal responsibility for figuring out what they themselves can contribute to a solution.

Step 3: Generate solution options.

Laurie: Well, later this morning I could walk down the street and pick up menus from those restaurants on the corner. If we order out, that would take care of food. We'd save the cooking time, too. And we could both start right away with the office boxes.

Tory: That would be great. I'd be glad to start by clearing the kitchen table so at least we can eat what you bring back. Then let's tackle the office starting with the box of music CD's.

Laurie: Great plan. Is there anything about it that's still unfinished?

Tory: Where do you think the boom box might be?

Laurie: Here it is. Hey, I'll try phoning for the takeout; that will be even faster.

Laurie and Tory used the win-win waltz successfully to reach agreement on a practical matter—what order to unpack in their new apartment. All kinds of controversies and decisions, little to large, can be settled collaboratively the same way.

Recognize the Three Steps

Clarity about the three steps of the win-win waltz can help to make your initial attempts at using this new skill easier. As you gain familiarity with the steps, you'll feel increasingly ready to try out the skill with your partner.

Note that each step contains one key component.

- Positions are preferences are the initial thoughts on what each of you would like to do. They may be expressed as concerns, but more often come in the form of solutions.

- Concerns are the reality factors, wishes, fears, and other dimensions of the problem to which a plan of action will need to be responsive.

- Solutions are plans of action.

Hone Your Skills

Successful win-win conflict resolution depends on being able to distinguish underlying concerns from solutions. Six of the comments below are concerns, and four are solutions, that is, action plans.

Statements	Concerns	Solutions
1. I think the children should go to summer camp.		✓
2. I want to take a family camping trip.		
3. I get overwhelmed when it's just me alone with the kids all day.		
4. It's important to me that we have plenty of time together as a family.		
5. I'm worried that we need honeymoon time as a couple.		

6. Let's hire a nanny.		
7. Last summer we spent far too much money.		
8. The kids need free time to enjoy playing together.		
9. Let's set aside two hours each day for the kids to hang out together.		
10. I'd like all of us to have a lot of time outdoors.		

Specific suggestions for summer plans in statements one, two, six, and nine were solutions, the rest enumerated underlying concerns.

In the following exercise, use your understanding of positions, concerns, and solutions to track which step of the waltz Cathy and Kevin are using. Circle the number of the step for each speaker

Which step(s) of the waltz is this?

Cathy: Kevin, I want to do some more exercises in our marriage skills workbook.   1 2 3

Kevin: I'd rather not tonight. We've been doing so much of the workbook that we haven't had time just to hang out together. That's what I'd like to do. Let's sit out on the balcony, light some candles ...   1 2 3

Cathy: We were off to a great start on the workbook, but lately we've done less. I'm concerned we won't finish the book if we don't stay focused on it. We are communicating so much better. I want to keep up the momentum.   1 2 3

Kevin: We do have a track record of starting things and not completing them—like our flower beds, well, dirt beds! I just want to be sure we also have some fun. I loved the bike trip we took last weekend.   1 2 3

Cathy: How can we keep the fun and also be sure we stick with the workbooks until we complete them?   1 2 3

Kevin: I've got a great idea. Let's toss the workbooks in our backpacks and head out on our bikes again this weekend. When we take biking breaks, we can put in workbook time.   1 2 3

Cathy: Fabulous. Let's bike out to that pond we heard about. I'll pack a picnic lunch, so we can eat while we study.   1 2 3

Kevin: I'm off to check the air in our tires.   1 2 3

As soon as Cathy and Kevin realize they differ, they immediately switch from talking about solutions—that is, plans of action—to exploring their underlying concerns. Once their concerns are clear, solutions flow creatively. Instead of their conflict yielding tension, it stimulates creative thinking, engenders enthusiasm, and ends up with learning plus a lovely day in the sunshine.

Practice with Your Partner

Read again through the blank worksheet. Copy or draw up extra copies of the worksheet for this exercise and for future use.

Imagine yourselves as the following couples. Practice by solving their conflicts, filling in a separate worksheet for each situation. Use your imagination to create concerns and solutions for each scenario. Make up details as if you are writing a play.

- Jennifer wants to shop at the mall and Bennett wants to go work out together.

- Ariel wants to take a trip by motorcycle. Tim would prefer to use regular bikes.

- Teresa doesn't like TV and wants to watch it less. Brian, however, loves watching sports.

- Pete wants to take a nap. Georgette wants to go before the stores close to look together at a sofa she would like to buy.

- Rose wants to invest in the stock market and Abram thinks it's too risky.

Conflict Resolution and Shared Decision-Making

Marriage entails making many decisions together. Every decision is a potential conflict. Whereas one person can fairly easily decide what time to eat dinner, what car to buy, and how high to hang pictures on the walls, two people addressing decisions together becomes more complicated. Tension is likely to rise. No one wants to lose out on getting what they want.

Interestingly, successful conflict resolution and shared decision making are one and the same. They proceed along the same three steps. What differs is just the initial tone. We tend to label the process *conflict resolution* if differences have created adversarial stances or an argument. If dialogue from the outset has been cooperative, the three win-win steps beaome shared decision-making.

Decisions Focus on the Future

All decisions are inherently future oriented. The future under discussion may be close—as close as the next few minutes. For instance, "Shall we stay at the party longer or go home now?" Sometimes, by contrast, shared decision-making looks ahead to the distant future. "Shall we aim to travel to Africa in five years if we can save enough to take a month off from our jobs?"

Practice with Your Partner

What decisions, small or large, do you have ahead in your life? List two, preferably fairly easy ones.

1. _____

2. _____

Taking one of these decisions at a time, practice your shared decision-making skills. Use the win-win waltz worksheet to help you to stay on track.

Hint: If you become stuck, put aside this decision until you have completed the next chapter on conflict-resolution tips and traps to avoid. Work on an easier decision for now.

After you have completed these decision-making experiments, answer the following questions.

- How clear were you about distinguishing among mutual positions, concerns, and solutions?

- To what extent did the plan of action you agreed on by the end of step three feel genuinely satisfactory to both of you?

The hardest part of shared decision-making is recognizing when to use it. Anytime you need to make a plan or decide what you will do about something, use the win-win waltz. Any time one of you wants one thing and the other wants something else, use the win-win waltz. Any time you become aware of rising tensions, check if a decision is at stake. Some tensions stem from communication glitches or from behavior that seemed to be out-of-bounds. Most of the rest of the time, though, tensions are signs of conflict, and conflict means that you need to make a shared win-win waltz decision.

From "Your Way" or "My Way" to "Our Way"

Every adult has had a childhood. When you were growing up, your family had routines for the business of living together—ways of handling cooking and cleaning, of enjoying and disputing with each other, of spending and saving, and of handling all the details of life as a family. In addition, if you lived on your own for a period of time before you were married, you will already have created some patterns of your own for the business of living.

Now comes the dilemma. Marriage involves two adults, each of whom grew up with his or her own prior routines. That means that you as a couple need to develop shared ways of proceeding. Again and again, you will need to sort out whether to use your way, your spouse's way, or a new *our way* for each aspect of living together.

The win-win waltz can guide creative shared decision making in each arena of living together where your visions differ: "Shall we keep the house spotless like my mother did, or let the clutter and dust build up until Saturday morning, cleaning once a week like your mother did?" "Shall we save like your folks did or spend as I like to?"

Practice with Your Partner

Practice your skills at choreographing win-win decisions as a couple by completing the following chart together. Fill in the third column together to create a mutual plan.

Hint: Use your win-win worksheet!

Dilemma	My Way	My Spouse's Way	Our Way
How do you fold towels?			
What needs to be done to clean up after dinner?			
How do you celebrate birthdays?			
How do you maintain a car?			
How do you keep a checkbook?			

Talk Together

Every couple has some areas where your preferred notions of how to handle the routines of daily life are somewhat different. Identify an area where you differ.

Situation:

1. How have you addressed this dilemma in the past?

2. Use the win-win waltz to create an *our way.*

3. How was this discussion the same or different from how you have talked about this difference in the past?

4. Now try addressing the second issue.

Agreement on how you will handle the details of life makes for smoother lives together. Marriages may be made in heaven, but the details definitely need to be worked out on earth.

"Fix-It" Talk

Shared-decision making helps couples approach decisions about how to handle upcoming situations as cooperative partners. *Fix-it talk* is our term for discussions designed to rectify problematic ongoing situations. This variation of the win-win waltz helps you remain constructive when you feel frustrated.

You can tell when a problem needs fixing because you will experience unpleasant feelings like irritation, annoyance, or anxiety. These moments of negative feelings are inevitable. As we have said repeatedly in this chapter, marriage involves two of you, which is a setup for conflict. In addition, life inherently involves change, and change means that routines that worked yesterday may no longer work today.

Fix-it talk prefaces the win-win waltz with two steps.

- **Step 1: Listen to a feeling.** Your feelings may talk in quiet voices. Take them seriously nonetheless.

- **Step 2: Describe the dilemma evoking those feelings.** When your spouse has the same information about the situation that you have, cooperation toward fixing the problem is most likely.

These two preliminary steps set the stage for launching into the win-win waltz.

To begin the waltz steps, use your request skills. A request, as we talked about in chapter 1, is a *would like to* followed by a question about your spouse's view on the matter. Saying your *would like to* (remember, *not* a "would like *you* to") and asking your spouse *how* or *what* he or she feels about the matter accomplishes step one of the win-win waltz, expressing initial action preferences. Exploring underlying concerns and generating solution options then can follow.

In the following example, Julia uses fix-it talk skillfully.

Step 1: Listen to your feeling

Julia: (listens to a feeling, saying to herself) If I'm annoyed at Jon I guess we need to talk. (aloud) I've been feeling down lately. I'd like to talk it over with you. Is now okay?

Step 2: Describe the dilemma

Julia: Since my Mom's been sick, I haven't been exercising. I'm also feeling extremely overloaded. I'm feeling like I need a teammate.

Win-Win Waltz

Julia: I'd love it if you could trade off some with me on visiting Mom in the hospital. Moving her from the hospital, plus all her belongings from her apartment, to a senior care facility is also going to be a huge project. Probably that will begin in several days. I'd love it if we could both give up on our daily exercise times for the next week to resettle her. How would you feel about that?

Jon is able to suggest an alternative plan—taking some time off from his work. He verbalizes his main concern—with his high cholesterol, any time away from his daily exercise regime scares him. With both of their concerns spelled out, Julia's for help and

Jon's for his heart, they map a plan for accomplishing together crisis care for the older generation.

Don't Force It

While your negative feelings signal helpfully that something has gone awry, they can also impel you to try to force solutions on your spouse instead of talking cooperatively. In the face of virtually any such difficult moment, you can either talk cooperatively together to fix the problem or try to force changes on your spouse.

Fix-it talk acknowledges negative feelings, but then deals with the situation cooperatively, without criticism or anger.

Force-it talk, by contrast, is decision making by domination. Force-it talk utilizes crossovers, criticism, and insistence to get your way. Force-it talk is controlling, focused on making your spouse do what you want. In its mild forms, as persuasion or repetitive insistence, force-it talk yields unpleasantness. In extremes, force-it talk lies at the heart of abusive behavior. Recognizing force-it talk therefore is important in keeping your relationship emotionally healthy.

Hone Your Skills

Learn to avoid forcing decisions by recognizing common force-it strategies. Below, the left column lists nine common versions of force-it talking. The right column contains an example of each type of mistaken strategy. Place the number for the type of mistake from the left column into the blanks on the right. Have you ever resorted to using any of these strategies?

Force-it strategies	Examples
1. Blame instead of insights	# _____ Either we get me a computer or I'm quitting my part-time job.
2. Criticism instead of requests	# _____ I'm getting a new computer. That's that.
3. Crossovers instead of I-messages	# _____ You're hardly perfect. You make all kinds of mistakes about what hardware you need.
4. Debate instead of asking *how* and *what* questions	# _____ It's your fault. You only buy what you want, not what I want or need.
5. Pleading instead of listening to learn	# _____ Please let's get a new computer. Please honey. Please, it's really critical.

6. Manipulation by guilt instead of saying concerns	# ____ That computer's fine. No it's not. Yes it is.
7. Insisting instead of exploring your spouse's concerns	# ____ If you don't agree, I won't talk to you.
8. Punishment instead of problem-solving.	# ____ You must be thinking that this is a frivolous expenditure.
9. Threats instead of seeking win-win solutions	# ____ Your response sure doesn't feel very supportive. If you really cared about me, you'd support me on this.

Force-it talk may initially feel like it gets you your way, but it generally proves counterproductive in the long run. Even small bits of force-it talk can prove corrosive.

Force-it talk	Fix-it talk
feels bullying	feels cooperative
spreads ill will and invites anger	soothes and reduces tensions
erodes love and intimacy	increases intimacy and love
creates ineffective solutions with one person unsatisfied or resentful	creates effective solutions that leave both people pleased

Fix-It Talk Stays Constructive

Fix-it talk helps you stay constructive at times when irritation might tempt you to complain or criticize. When problems need fixing, there is no room for slippage away from effective habits of communicating. Fix-it talk, like all win-win waltzing,

- sticks with I-messages
- stays focused on the problem, not the person
- converts potential *don't like* messages to *would like to* messages
- avoids the negativity of blame, complaints, or criticisms

The following dialogue illustrates how fix-it talk brings about win-win problem-solving in a particularly provocative situation. Can you sense when Renee is slipping and when she is constructive?

Frank and Renee's roof is leaking. It is pouring rain and they are watching the drips falling into a bucket on their new Persian carpet.

Step 1: Listen to your feelings.

Renee: *(to herself)* My irritation is there to tell me I need to speak up before I get really mad and explode.

Renee: *(aloud)* Frank, I'm very worried about our new rug. Let's talk.

Step 2: Describe the dilemma.

Renee: *(to herself)* I'm furious at Frank. He told me he fixed the roof and that it would be fine. He insisted he could save money repairing it himself, that we didn't need to call a roofer. He was wrong, and now we're paying the price. He was foolish. The carpet is going to get ruined! Oops. I'm focusing on Frank, but he's not the problem. The rain on the carpet is the problem.

Renee: *(aloud)* Frank, as that rain is coming into our living room harder and harder, I'm getting frantic. If we weren't here to keep dumping the bucket, our new carpet would have been ruined. I know that you tried to patch the roof last week, but it doesn't seem to have worked. We need to do something.

Win-win waltz, starting with a request.

Renee: Frank, I appreciate your help figuring out what to do. I would like to save the rug. Shall I make an emergency call to a professional roofer? Or maybe can you go up now and fix the roof again?

Frank: We don't have money for professionals; that just isn't an option. I can't believe I just patched that roof last week and now it's leaking again. Darn! I hate the thought of another day of trying to hammer nails in the rain! I really don't want to have to go up on the roof again in a storm. We need to protect the carpet, but I'm stymied.

Renee: Okay. You don't want to spend money or to have to hammer in the rain. I want to make sure the carpets are safe. What if I roll up the new carpet? We could put it in the other room for now. I'll keep manning buckets. Then, when the rain clears up, would you repatch the roof?

Frank: That's a good idea. The rain has to end sometime. Once it's sunny outside again, I bet I could get a friend to come over and help. I'd enjoy the work more that way, and maybe Karl or Joe would know how to fix what I obviously didn't do successfully last time.

Renee: Great! I'd be glad to get the grill going while you guys fix the roof. Burgers with fresh tomatoes from the garden?

In the example above, Renee struggled to avoid criticizing Frank. She began to upset herself with overgeneralized negative thoughts about him, but then succeeded in switching to the steps of fix-it talk:

- regarding her annoyance as a sign that a problem needs fixing

- turning from negative thinking about Frank to neutral descriptions of the problem

- launching win-win problem solving with a *would like*

Identify Fix-It Talk Moments

Like shared decision-making, the hardest part of fix-it talk tends to be realizing when you need to use it. In general, the tip-off that a problem needs fixing is feeling anxious or irritated.

Practice with Your Partner

How do you know that it's time to use fix-it talk? The following chart gives some types of situations that may be familiar to you. Work together to think of examples from your relationship for each situation.

Situation	Example	Examples from your marriage
You or your spouse have been doing things one way and you would like to make a change in the pattern, a change in your system for handling that situation.	When you are talking on the phone, your spouse talks to you, suggesting things to say.	1. 2. 3.
A new circumstance has arisen.	An unexpected expense puts you under financial pressure.	1. 2. 3.
Something your spouse does frustrates you.	Your spouse leaves lights on all night, wasting electricity.	1. 2. 3.

Look back over the chart together. Select a situation that each of you would like to address. Use fix-it talk to work together to find a new solution for this situation. Check off each step below as you do it.

Hint: Pick situations that feel approachable. You may need the advanced skills in the next chapter to resolve the more challenging ones.

Your situation: _____

_____ Listen to your feelings.

_____ Explain the situation.

_____ Express initial preferences.

_____ Explore underlying concerns.

_____ Generate solution options.

Your spouse's situation: _____

_____ Listen to your feelings.

_____ Explain the situation.

_____ Express initial preferences.

_____ Explore underlying concerns.

_____ Generate solution options.

The more quickly you notice fix-it talk opportunities, the more smoothly your household will run. Problems no longer will fester. As you become accustomed to using fix-it talk, dilemmas which otherwise would have been sore points become gratifying challenges.

Summing Up and Moving On

You now have learned the skills that enable couples to make decisions in a shared manner. You have learned to resolve differences about household routines by creating an *our way*. You have learned how small feelings, especially those of annoyance, can help you launch fix-it talk and have learned to recognize signs of unconstructive force-it talk.

The next chapter offers additional tips to enhance your win-win waltz effectiveness. It suggests traps to avoid. And it warns you of what happens when couples do not use win-win skills.

CHAPTER 9

Win-Win Tips,
Traps, and Costs

Win-win conflict resolution sometimes takes additional know-how to flow to a solution you both feel good about. This chapter offers advanced skills that can increase your effectiveness with the three basic steps of the win-win waltz.

Is all this learning worth the effort? Much of what is dysfunctional in couples and families boils down to deficits in conflict resolution. When differences arise in dysfunctional relationships, spouses dominate each other, get depressed, drink, or avoid one another. Learning to settle disagreements with win-win dialogue has a huge payoff!

Tips

At the start, you may feel more like a toddler wobbling across the floor than an accomplished win-win dancer. The following additional tips can make the steps flow more effectively.

- **Identify what you would like to do, not just what you don't want.** Saying what you don't want, you have already learned, is generally ineffective and off-putting. Negativity tends similarly to put a damper on win-win problem solving. By contrast, saying what you would like to do guides the way to effective solutions. "I don't want to just stay home this summer" is less effective than "I'd like to travel some this summer, especially to visit someplace exotic."

- **The more specifics, the better.** In chapter 5 you learned how specifics facilitate building mutual understanding. Thought you might think that giving a lot of specifics would make solution-building harder. In fact, giving more details about your concerns actually increases the likelihood of finding a solution. The expression, "I'd like to fix up the house," right away becomes clearer if you also say, "I'd like to get the outside of the house painted while the weather is still good; we can paint indoors in the winter."

- **Think in terms of solution sets.** Effective solutions often involve a "solution set." Rather than one simple answer, the plan may need multiple components, each responsive to different concerns. A simple solution to summer planning might be, "Let's take a trip." A solution set might be, "Let's take a trip to somewhere exotic, repaint the house on weekends, and join a softball league."

- **Retracing steps can be helpful.** As you proceed through the three steps, odds are that once you get to step three, devising solutions, you will find that some of the solution ideas raise additional concerns. In fact, the win-win waltz steps often go one, two, three, two, three—back to exploring concerns, creating new solution ideas, and then maybe even back again to exploring concerns, before a thoroughly good solution set emerges.

Practice with Your Partner

You and your spouse may encounter bumpy spots as you role-play the following shared decision-making situations. Use the above tips to help you out.

- You want to keep your beloved old car and your spouse wants to replace it with something more reliable.

- You want to have a large family and your spouse wants a small one.

As you finish role-playing each situation, go over the following tip list to check if you succeeded in using each suggestion. If you missed any, practice them by continuing your discussion.

- Did you each express your initial suggestions as *would like to* requests?

- As you explored your underlying concerns, did you include enough specifics?

- Did you create a solution set, or just a simple one-part solution?

- Did you retrace your steps, returning to explore more underlying concerns, after you had generated your first few suggestions?

Difficult Dilemmas

Some dilemmas are inherently difficult. They may involve issues of major importance, multiple complicated factors, or quite different starting visions. In these cases especially, the following additional ideas can help.

- **Step back and summarize.** A summary of all the concerns each of you has listed so far can help in many ways. Summaries gather the concerns together, clarifying your shared perspective. Summaries propel movement from step two, exploring underlying concerns, to step three, creating solutions. Summaries consolidate bilateral listening so both of you feel that all the concerns of both of you matter. Summaries often stimulate breakthroughs to new solution ideas. Summaries are also a helpful cure for slipping into adversarial stances. You might want to review the section on summaries in chapter 5.

- **Identify the core concerns.** When a decision is particularly complex with multiple variables, identify which concern stands out as most important. Find a solution that is responsive to this one concern. Then build the rest of the solution set around this basic solution. For example, if you are looking for a house to buy, the most important concern may be proximity to your work. The other dimensions—spaciousness, sunlight, kitchen counter space, cost, and so on—become second-tier factors, also vital in the solution-building process, but only after you have limited your housing search to neighborhoods close to your work.

- **Think outside the box.** To find solutions responsive to all of the concerns on your joint list, consider resources beyond the two of you. For instance, if the question is who will mow the lawn, consider hiring the teenager down the block. Consider also reducing the lawn in half by putting in other groundcover. Or buy sheep. To find creative solutions, brainstorm together. Thinking of as many options as you can, good or bad, frees up your mind. The most outrageous ideas, if you let yourselves tinker with them, sometimes turn out to work well.

- **Make time your ally.** Identify your concerns, brainstorm on a few solutions, and then put the problem aside for a bit. Sleep on it, and address the issue again another day. Time lets additional important dimensions bubble up. Time distills those concerns that are primary. Time can yield surprisingly good solutions.

- **Take a hike.** Especially on high-stakes decisions, tensions are likely to arise. Tension interferes with creativity. You will both think better if you talk as you walk together, rock in rocking chairs, or sit by a fire. Gentle movement and a lovely environment can help to keep you maximally open and creative.

Hone Your Skills

Below is a dialogue between spouses who are facing a difficult upcoming decision.

Number the steps of the win-win waltz as they occur in each comment. Some comments may need two numbers, as they may include two steps. Notice this couple's strong win-win skills. They keep one list of concerns, explore underlying concerns, look for solution sets, and repeat steps as needed.

Alexandra and Sebastian are trying to decide where to raise their family.

Step # _____   *Alexandra:* I'd really like to move back to Brazil.

Step # _____   *Sebastian:* I guess when I think about raising kids, I'd like them to grow up on a ranch like I did, so I always assumed we'd stay in Montana.

Step # _____   *Alexandra:* So let's see, what makes me want to go back to Brazil? Well, to begin with, I still struggle with English, and your Portuguese is so good! Plus, I hate the cold dark winters around here. I end up so depressed.

Step # _____   *Sebastian:* And for me, the ranch was a lifestyle where it was safe for kids to run around alone. I have this image of our kids being outside all day, playing with each other, and doing things like raising animals—not plugged into the TV.

Step # _____   *Alexandra:* Well, maybe we could live somewhere in rural Brazil?

Step # _____   *Sebastian:* In theory that sounds like it meets all the criteria, but it just doesn't appeal to me. There must be more pulling at me. I guess I underestimated how much I'd like to be near my parents. Now that I think about it, I'm really worried that my parents are going to need my help managing the ranch in the not-too-distant future.

Step # _____   *Alexandra:* And as I think about it, I have some additional fears. In Brazil my college degree counts for something. I'm worried that there isn't much I will be able to do here with a degree in Portuguese literature.

Before they get stuck, help Sebastian and Alexandra to summarize their concerns.

1. _____

2. _____

3. _____

4. _____

5. _____

6. _____

7. _____

Decide for Alexandra which concern is most pressing for her. _____

_____

_____

Decide for Sebastian which concern is most pressing for him. _____

_____

_____

Starting with these most pressing concerns, devise a solution set that might leave both Alexandra and Sebastian feeling satisfied. (Hint: This is a time for creativity and thinking outside of the box!) _____

_____

_____

_____

_____

Tips for Fix-It Talk Success

The talking, listening, and dialogue skills you learned in the first chapters of this book make a big difference with win-win waltzing. In fix-it talk, for instance, heeding your feelings, verbalizing them, and listening to your partner's feelings enable you to get started improving the situation.

Hone Your Skills

Think back to a recent moment when there was a situation in your relationship that needed fixing. You might want to use one of the more challenging situations you've recently identified. Close your eyes and recall what happened when you or your spouse tried to address the problem.

Now read through the following fix-it talk and win-win waltz pointers. As you read through the list, place a check next to each technique that you used in the discussion you just visualized.

Situation: _____

Fix-it step 1: Listen to your feelings.

____ Treasure small feelings. Hear even your tiny grumbles and faint whispers of concerns.

____ Speak up when feelings are subtle, before the situation worsens or your annoyance builds.

Fix-it step 2: Describe the dilemma.

____ Say it. If your spouse has the information you have, your reactions are more likely to be similar.

____ Be sure you are simply describing—not insisting, convincing, criticizing, blaming, or in any other way trying to force your perspective.

Do the win-win waltz:

____ Keep your initial request positive. Avoid complaints like "You should have. . . ."

_____ Keep your _would like to_ about _you_—"I'd like to . . . ." Avoid "I'd like _you_ to . . ." directives for your spouse.

_____ Be sure your request includes a question asking for your spouse's viewpoint.

_____ Focus on solving the problem, not on blaming.

_____ Throughout your discussion, be especially careful to listen to learn. Listen for what's right, makes sense, or is useful in what you are hearing.

_____ Digest aloud what you hear, and then add your perspective.

_____ As you move to exploring solutions, stay focused on what you can do. Let your spouse focus on what he or she can do.

_____ Be sure your plan of action responds to all the concerns each of you have expressed.

Are some boxes still unchecked? Here is your opportunity to rewrite this discussion in a way that will allow you to check off all of the boxes.

Imagine that some other couple, Fitz and Mabel, are in the exact same situation as you. Fitz and Mabel are experts at fix-it talk. They use all of the tips above, plus those advanced tips you have learned earlier in this chapter as well. Use the lines below to write a dialogue between Fitz and Mabel about the issue you identified. If you need more space, continue on another piece of paper.

Fitz: _____

_____

Mabel: _____

_____

Fitz: _____

_____

Mabel: _____

_____

Fitz: _____

_____

Mabel: _____

_____

Fitz: _____

_____

Mabel: _____

_____

Talk Together

Share your Fitz and Mabel dialogue with your spouse, and then answer the following questions together. What did Fitz and Mabel do that seemed especially helpful? How did these techniques change the tone and outcome of the discussion? What have each of you learned for next time you need to use fix-it talk?

Traps to Avoid

When you first try the win-win waltz, you or your spouse may become discouraged. You may be tempted to say, "That win-win waltz doesn't work." Usually, your frustrations will come from getting stuck in one of the following traps:

- attachment to a particular solution

- criticizing your spouse's concerns

- premature closure

Avoid Attachment to Any One Solution

If one of you becomes overly attached to one specific solution, arguing for that solution instead of exploring concerns, the win-win-waltz will grind to a halt.

Gertrude: I really want to rent a movie tonight.

George: I'd rather do something active.

Gertrude: Renting a movie is a way better idea.

George: I was thinking that a brisk walk to watch the sunset in the park would be fun.

Gertrude: Renting a movie is the only thing I want to do.

Hone Your Skills

You can release an attachment to a particular solution by switching to exploring concerns. Hint: Good *how* and *what* questions can facilitate the switch from solutions to concerns.

Gertrude: I really want to rent a movie tonight.

George: _____

_____

Gertrude: _____

_____

George: _____

_____

Gertrude: _____

_____

Avoid Criticizing Concerns

As you learned earlier in this book, feedback can be helpful, but criticism is risky. In the context of shared problem solving, criticizing your spouse's concerns indicates you are invalidating instead of seeking to understand what matters to him or her. Essential information gets lost that way, and so does goodwill. Criticizing your spouse's concerns derails win-win waltzing.

Gertrude: I'd like us to go see a financial planner.

George: What a waste of time. Our finances our fine.

Gertrude: I know we're okay now, but I'm worried about the future. What if one of us loses our job?

George: Come on, we've never had a problem finding good jobs. A financial planner would just meddle in our business.

Gertrude: No really, I think we might learn something helpful.

While George and Gertrude don't use the word but, their pattern of criticizing rather than listening to what each other says has the same impact. They spin their wheels in frustrating dialogue with no forward movement.

You can offer differing views. Just be sure first to listen to learn. After you have heard, you understand, and you have conveyed what you understand of your spouse's concern, then you can add your different perspective. That way dialogue moves forward, accumulating mutual understanding.

Hone Your Skills

George and Gertrude were unable to move forward with win-win dialogue because they criticized each other's concerns instead of trying to understand them. Release them from their trap by helping them to listen to learn, digest aloud, and then add their concerns with *yes, and.* If they are not clear what they could agree with, help them ask *how* or *what* questions.

Gertrude: I'd like us to go see a financial planner.

George: _____

_____

Gertrude: _____

_____

George: _____

_____

Gertrude: _____

George: _____

Money is on most couples' lists of high-conflict topics. It requires several skills to keep the talking safe.

With respectful listening instead of critical responses, Gertrude and George can talk productively. Did your version of George and Gertrude's dialogue look something like this?

George: It seems to me our finances are fine. What did you have in mind that you thought we should see a planner?

Gertrude: I know we're okay now....

George: That's true.

Gertrude: My friend Lisa got fired yesterday. I could lose my job too.

George: Your right. I'm glad both of us bring in the bacon, so if one of us loses our job we can still squeeze by.

Gertrude: A planner could give us ideas on how to plan for hard times.

George: You may be right. I'm certainly not an expert in investment strategy. Still, I'm worried a planner would meddle in our business.

Gertrude: I agree, I certainly don't want to feel like someone else is controlling our purse. At the same time, I'd be less anxious if we learned more.

If your spouse offers information that seems wrong or ideas that make no sense to you, ask for more information. You may be delightfully surprised at what you hear!

Avoid Premature Closure

Premature closure occurs if you decide on a plan of action when you needed to spend more time exploring underlying concerns. Though you both may have agreed to a solution, premature closure eventually results in one or both of you feeling less than satisfied. The solution for avoiding premature closure is easy—before ending the conversation, ask if everything feels resolved: "Are there any little pieces of this that still feel unfinished?"

Gertrude: I know that when we planned this vacation, we were both really excited to drive cross-country, but I'm starting to worry that it's too much driving.

George: Well, I really wanted to drive, but we could just fly instead.

Gertrude: Okay.

        (Then, after the vacation)

George: I'm so disappointed we didn't get to see any little towns. All we did was fly from big city to big city.

Gertrude: You wanted to drive so we could see little towns? I had no idea. I would have loved to rent a car in some cities and get out into the countryside. Boy, I wish we had talked that through more!

Hone Your Skills

Release the trap by checking for closure. Ask if everything feels resolved.

Gertrude: I'm starting to worry that our vacation will have too much driving.

George: Let's fly instead.

Gertrude: Okay. Let's fly. Are there any pieces of this that still feel unfinished?

George: _____

_____

Gertrude: _____

_____

George: _____

_____

In sum, if your win-win waltzing slows to a halt, restart the dialogue by

1. exploring concerns if you were attaching to positions

2. responding with *yes, and* instead of criticism of each other's concerns

3. ending by checking that you both feel fully satisfied with the decision: "Are there any little peices of this that still feel unfinished."

Costs of Conflict

All couples consciously or unconsciously develop systems for resolving their differences. They may fight for a while and then drop the issue. They may decide in favor of the person who insists most. They may take turns with who gets their way. Or both spouses may compromise, giving up some of what they want.

Anger, depression, anxiety, and addictive patterns can emerge as by-products of flawed conflict resolution. These negative emotional downsides of less than win-win conflict-resolution strategies can become especially problematic when

- the topic about which decisions have been made is one of major import

- decision making drags on without clear outcomes

- the decision is made in favor of one of you and is inadequately responsive to deeply felt concerns of the other

Five Conflict-Resolution Patterns

A wide range of conflict-resolution styles can all be traced to permutations and combinations of just five patterns (listed below). Only the last one really works.

Conflict Option	Emotion	Purpose	Cost or Outcome
1. **Fight** Use force-it talk.	anger	to get what you want and resist another solution	Spouse will be mad, resentful, or depressed in response.
2. **Freeze** Delay talking.	anxiety	to avoid fighting	Tension; chronic indecision; the dilemma doesn't get solved.
3. **Flight** Avoid the topic with distraction by drugs or alcohol.	addictive behaviors instead of feelings	to avoid fighting and anxiety	The dilemma doesn't get solved; plus the alcohol or other addictions create additional problems.
4. **Yield** Give up.	depression	to be nice and to sustain the relationship	Depression is no fun, and neither is living with a depressed partner.
5. **The Win-Win Waltz**	pleasure	to please both of you	No costs. Solve the problem and enjoy shared well-being.

Hone Your Skills

The following scenario could have many endings, depending on how Victor and Linda handle conflict.

Victor lost his job. The plant was closing. The company did offer him a similar managerial position in its Chicago plants, however. Victor said to Linda, "I feel desperate. I really want to take the job." Linda did not want to move away from her friends and family, but she said nothing. Instead, she began packing, trying to hide her tears. She felt she had no choice.

Which pattern does this exemplify? _____

Imagine yourself as Linda: How would you feel? _____

What outcome is likely from this way of handling conflict? _____

_____

> *Linda turned to Victor and snapped forcefully, "You can't make me move. You're not going to boss me. I'm staying here."*

Which pattern does this exemplify? _____

Imagine yourself as Linda: What emotion would you be feeling? _____

Imagine yourself as Victor: How would you feel? _____

What outcome is likely from this way of handling conflict? _____

_____

> *Victor couldn't face his sadness at the ending of his job, and dreaded hearing Linda's reaction. He began stopping at a bar driving home from work.*

Which pattern does this exemplify? _____

What outcome is likely from this way of handling conflict? _____

_____

> *Victor told Linda about the plant closing, but didn't discuss the move. He was afraid she would be angry. He kept it secret for a month.*

Imagine yourself as Victor: How would you feel? _____

What outcome is likely from this way of handling conflict? _____

_____

> *Victor told Linda that he wants to take the job. Linda responded: "I'm worried I would really miss my friends if we moved so far, far away. Let's see if we can figure out a plan that would work for us both."*

Which pattern does this exemplify? _____

What are the results? _____

_____

How spouses make decisions together determines how they will feel. The examples above illustrate how Linda and Victor can end up feeling depressed, angry, addicted, then anxious—and then comfortable, enjoying ongoing feelings of well-being.

Self-Reflection

Self-reflection about the extent to which you have been using any of the four negative conflict-resolution strategies above is important. You cannot fix what you are not seeing.

Think back on times when you have felt angry, been anxious, become depressed, or avoided a situation by using an addiction. Recall if you can, the situation that these negative feelings or addictive actions were responding to. Can you identify the underlying conflict and the conflict pattern that led to your symptoms?

Examine Your Background

Think of times when you have used each of the conflict options described above. Note these instances in the chart below with brief names like, "the kitchen table battle" or "the in-laws issue." Then note the outcomes of each strategy.

Conflict Option	Feeling	Situations	Costs or Outcomes
1. **Fight**	anger		
2. **Freeze**	anxiety		
3. **Flight**	addictive behaviors; no feelings		

4. **Yield**	depression		
5. **The Win-Win Waltz**	pleasure		

Summing Up and Moving On

The bottom line is that solving conflicts in ways other than by the win-win waltz can prove to be highly emotionally expensive, and costly for the relationship as well. The good news is that by practicing win-win problem solving, plus from time to time reviewing the tips and traps in this chapter, your future can be bright.

Realistically, it takes time to build consistency to the point that you virtually always use these cooperative patterns. Occasional upsets may occur. The next chapter teaches how to get back on track after they do.

CHAPTER 10

Handling Upsets

What you have learned so far about cooperative talking and listening, safe anger expression, and win-win problem solving will help you to handle most potentially contentious situations with constructive dialogue. With practice, you can become a virtually fight-free couple as both of you become solid with your new skills. Even then, you still will need to be totally determined to talk, not tiff, when you are tired or hungry, one of you slips in your skills, or you bump up against sensitive issues.

Yet, there will inevitably be some times when feelings are hurt or mishaps occur. The skills in this chapter on cleanup procedures ensure that if, for whatever reason, you and your spouse do begin to face off like injured adversaries, you can restore your sense of cooperative partnership.

This chapter concludes with an important warning. You can prevent major crises in your marriage by refraining from the three main creators of major marriage problems—affairs, addictions, and abusive anger. Avoid or immediately end these deal breakers if you want your marriage to remain loving and lasting.

After Upsets

What can you do if a cooperative dialogue slips into argument, erupts in anger, and one or both of you makes a mess?

Three skills, intertwined, can enable you to conclude even your most difficult situations with constructive understandings and a return of harmony.

- Figure out what happened by putting your perspectives together like the pieces of a puzzle.

- Find out what you missed instead of looking to blame or find fault.

- Apologize.

After upsets, even small ones, cleaning up the toxic spills helps you to resume an affectionate and mutually appreciative relationship. Best of all, by learning from upsets, you can lower the likelihood of a recurrence in the future.

What Doesn't Work

If you take a fall and bloody a white shirt, trying to clean the spot by pouring hot water on it will set the stain, making it more difficult to remove.

Unfortunately, couples may utilize similarly mistaken methods to clean up after marriage spills. Trying to heal from an upsetting incident by returning hurt for hurt, for instance, only creates more upset.

All of the responses in the box below make matters worse. Draw a line between each mistaken cleanup strategy and the example that illustrates it.

Mistaken strategies   Examples

1. Blame
    a. You shouldn't have embarrassed me with that snide comment at the party!

2. Punish
    b. I hate that you're always saying things that embarrass me.

3. Complain
    c. I think about how mad at you I am all day at my desk at work.

4. Resent
    d. It's your fault that people don't invite us to go out with them.

5. Humiliate
    e. After what you did, I'm not talking with you for a week.

6. Criticize
    f. What kind of total dunce would say that? You idiot!

7. Name-call
    g. (sarcastically, in front of others) That was real bright. No wonder you lost your job, with comments like that.*

Perhaps the most damaging response to upsets is threatening divorce. Thinking about divorce and, worse, threatening divorce increases the likelihood of divorce. Agreement from the outset never to threaten with the D-word can help to prevent this insecurity from ever being introduced into your household.

---

*   Anser key: 1-d; 2-e; 3-b; 4-c; 5-g; 6-a; 7-f.

Knowing what doesn't work is a start. The following exercises will give you better strategies for cleaning up.

Put Together the Puzzle

After a distressing incident, figuring out what happened is a first step. You know what you did and felt, but that is only half the story. To figure out a full picture of what happened, you also need to hear your spouse's perspective. Both pieces are necessary to complete the puzzle.

To put together the full picture of what happened, each of you relates what you experienced—what you did, thought, and felt—during the incident. No one is looking to blame or attribute fault—just to understand the full picture.

Putting together how the upset occurred requires absolute adherence to the no crossovers rule. Each of you is responsible for saying only what you experienced in the incident—avoiding comments about what your spouse may have thought, felt, or done. Just describe your own experience. Putting both your and your spouse's pieces of the puzzle together yields the big picture.

Hone Your Skills

Lynn is angry at Ollie for laughing at her when she was upset. Read their different accounts of the incident below. Then write what each learned from listening to the other.

Ollie and Lynn had been walking in the woods.

Lynn: We were hiking along in the woods and I saw a deer grazing. We had been chatting, so I assumed you would notice when it was suddenly quiet and turn around to see why I had stopped. When you didn't stop, I didn't want to holler because that would have scared away the deer. But when I was ready to go again, you were nowhere to be seen. I raced along as fast as I could to try to catch up. Then the trail forked, and I had no idea which way to go. I tried one path for a bit and didn't see you, so I turned around. At this point I was getting frantic that I would be lost in the woods and that you wouldn't find me. It was scary being alone. On top of that, the hiking had given me a blister. By the time I got back to the fork, I was crying. I was starting to think that maybe you had sped up just to get away from me, that you'd rather be hiking alone! Finally, after what seemed like forever, you came back. I couldn't believe you had the gall to laugh when you saw me. I was so hurt! So then I yelled at you for abandoning me.

Ollie: We were hiking along in the woods and chatting. Like it often does, the conversation lulled, and I began thinking about the addition we've been talking about putting on our house. It was nice to have a little bit of reflective time. My feet just carried me along. After a while, I was eager to share my ideas with you, and I started talking. I was surprised you didn't respond, so I turned around. When you weren't right behind me, I immediately doubled back to find you. When I saw you sitting on that rock, my first thought was what a beautiful wife I have, especially with what looked like small beads of sweat running down your face. I couldn't help but smile. It wasn't until you yelled at me that I had any idea you were upset. I couldn't figure out what could be wrong on such a beautiful day.

Lynn learned that Ollie: _____

_____

_____

_____

_____

Ollie learned that Lynn: _____

_____

_____

_____

_____

To put together the pieces of the puzzle, both of you need to trust that what your spouse is describing as his or her experience is true. Skepticism can undermine this strategy. Instead, listen to learn. Expect that in putting together a joint picture, you will end up taking in a new view of what happened.

One more hint: Like most dialogue, this strategy works best when it's highly interactive and neither of you dominates the conversation. This means that one of you says just a line or two about what you experienced, and the other then adds a similarly small piece or two of information. As you alternate adding information, you can piece together the story as you go along.

How do you know if you have been successful? The picture that emerges should offer you relief as you understand more fully what happened. In addition, the full picture sets you up for accomplishing the second phase of cleaning up after upsets: finding the missed piece that triggered the upset.

Solve the Mystery of What You Missed

Why do upsets occur? Cleaning up will proceed most productively if both of you assume from the outset that neither of you had bad intentions. No one did anything wrong or bad. Instead, the vast majority of upsets occur because of

- mistakes

- misunderstandings

- miscommunications

- missiles (when someone looses their temper and says something hurtful)

- misperceptions

- misestimations

- mishaps

Putting together the picture of what happened can enable you to discover what went wrong. As you identify what happened, any remaining rancor is likely to dissipate because neither of you was at fault or did anything deserving of criticism or blame. You just need to find the miss.

Hone Your Skills

Identify the misses in the following examples. We've helped you get started on the first one.

Gary was looking forward to going out to a dinner party with his wife Betsy. When he saw that the time was 5:30 and she wasn't home yet, he began to get annoyed.

What kinds of misses could have occurred? _____

_____*Misestimation—Betsy didn't realize how slow the traffic would be.*_____

_____*Mistake—*_____

_____*Miscommunication—*_____

_____

Betsy came home with three large bags that said Saks Fifth Avenue in big letters. Knowing how expensive the merchandise can be in this store, Gary began to feel angry. He thought they had agreed to cut back on expenses.

What kinds of misses could have occurred? _____

_____

_____

_____

_____

Betsy heard the phone ring, but since she was busy upstairs, she left the phone for Gary to pick up downstairs. When Gary didn't pick it up, Betsy was annoyed.

What kinds of misses could have occurred? _____

_____

_____

_____

_____

Hurt feelings are soothed, and anger from an upset can quickly dissipate, as you and your spouse put together the puzzle pieces of what happened. Mistakes, mishaps, and miscommunications are inevitable; figuring them out and how they occurred enables you to learn from them, sigh or laugh, and move on.

Apologies Take Six Steps

An apology, based on the understanding you have gained by putting together the puzzle pieces of what happened and finding the miss, completes the toxic cleanup process.

A full apology is actually a complex and powerful phenomenon. Everyone knows an apology can help after an upset. On the other hand, few people use the full power of apologies, especially, it seems, after marriage upsets. While an apology may take only a minute or two, a full apology actually includes six components.

Step 1: Express regret.

Step 2: Accept responsibility.

Step 3: Clarify nonintentionality.

Step 4: Explain the circumstances.

Step 5: Repair damages and prevent reoccurrences.

Step 6: Learn for the future.

In the example below, Ali apologizes for breaking his wife's favorite vase.

1. **Express regret:** "I'm so sorry that I broke your crystal vase!"

2. **Accept responsibility:** "I knocked the shelf when I was falling and now the vase is shattered."

3. **Clarify nonintentionality:** "I sure didn't mean to break it."

4. **Explain the circumstances:** "I brought in that small kitchen stepladder. I was reaching up to the shelf above the vase to take down my squash trophy to look what year I won the tournament. I slipped while I was climbing down and knocked the shelf."

5. **Repair damages:** "I'd really like to try to find a way to replace the vase. Do you have any ideas how? I know you really like that vase. I feel so bad about it."

6. **Learn for the future:** "That stepladder was cheap, but it's not safe. The steps are too small. I'll pick up a better one in the hardware store this weekend. And next time I climb up or down a ladder, I'm going to be extra careful—I'll take my time and think about what I'm doing instead of letting my mind scatter on twenty other things."

Hone Your Skills

Practice creating full apologies in the following situations.

You had a crazy day, trying to keep a major business deal alive. In the midst of the chaos, you forgot to pick up your daughter from day care. Your spouse is appalled when you come home unaware that your daughter is still at the child care center.

1. Express regret: _____

_____

2. Accept responsibility: _____

_____

_____

3. Clarify nonintentionality: _____

_____

4. Explain the circumstances: _____

_____

_____

5. Repair damages: _____

_____

_____

_____

6. Learn for the future: _____

_____

_____

_____

You bought theater tickets in advance for a musical you're excited to see. A week later, as the two of you are preparing for the event, you assure your spouse it begins at 8 o'clock. When you get to the theater at 7:45, the show has started.

1. Express regret: _____

_____

2. Accept responsibility: _____

_____

_____

3. Clarify nonintentionality: _____

_____

4. Explain the circumstances: _____

_____

_____

_____

5. Repair damages: _____

_____

_____

_____

6. Learn for the future: _____

_____

_____

_____

Apologies soothe by reassuring your spouse that you are willing to assume responsibility for your role in a mishap. Apologies do not say you are a bad person, at fault, or to blame, but only that you made an unfortunate and unintended error. You are taking credit for your part in the incident. Full closure occurs when you have figured out how to prevent a repeat of the problem.

For an apology to work it's full magic, however, your spouse must be receptive to soothing. It takes two to do this tango.

Likewise, when your spouse is apologizing, the burden of receptivity lies on you. You need to be willing to let go of angry urges to hurt back or punish, urges that can be seductive and yet prove counterproductive. Only by allowing yourself to be soothed with the balm of your spouse's apology can an unfortunate incident be fully resolved.

Strive for Double Apologies

A double apology contains mutual apologies with both of you acknowledging and expressing regret for your part in an upset, and both of you being receptive to the other's apology. Couples with skills for double apologies can clean up toxic spills with exceptional rapidity. They also end up with optimal learning to prevent similar upsets in the future. Couples with good double-apology skills are like gardening partners who pull weeds out with the roots so that the weeds seldom return.

Double apologies follow the same six steps; each partner takes a turn at each step.

Practice with Your Partner

Practice a double apology with your partner, using the following scenario. As you work through this pretend apology, check in your column after you complete each step. Be sure to alternate so you each complete each step before moving on to the next.

You and your spouse had been roller blading together, happily watching your children riding bikes ahead. One of you also is holding the leash to your dog. Suddenly, KABOOM. The skates collide and you both fly into the air. You bruise your knees. Your spouse's palms are bleeding.

Apology step	You did this	Your spouse did this
1. Express regret	_____	_____
2. Accept responsibility	_____	_____
3. Clarify nonintentionality	_____	_____
4. Explain the circumstances	_____	_____
5. Repair damages	_____	_____
6. Learn for the future	_____	_____

Double apologies acknowledge that neither of you meant to hurt the other. Instead of blaming each other, both of your energies go to understanding what happened, soothing each other, and preventing future mishaps.

Convert Curses to Blessings

By the time you take the last step in your double apology—learning for the future—already you both probably will be feeling considerably better. You have not yet finished thought. These last few minutes of the discussion are vital. They give you a chance to convert the lemon to lemonade, or, as some would say, to change the curse to a blessing.

To learn from the future, consider two questions.

1. What might you personally do differently in the future to avoid a repeat?

2. What can you as a couple restructure so that similar upsets will not reoccur?

As you think over how as a couple you could prevent these situations, you only are responsible for looking at your personal learning. Neither of you needs to think about what your spouse should change. Such suggestions would be crossovers. Beware of trespassing. If you each do your own reprogramming, plus some thinking about fixing your couple routines to prevent a repeat performance, that's plenty of learning.

Practice with Your Partner

Think back to the last time you and your spouse experienced an upset. In this exercise you will create a full double six-step apology. Then you will top it off with a discussion to figure out how to turn the sour-tasting upset into sweet lemonade. If you and your spouse think of different upsets, repeat the six steps below for both incidents.

Your upsetting incident: _____

Your spouse's upsetting incident: _____

Create a double six-step apology. Check off each step as you each do it. Be sure to alternate so you each complete each step before going on to the next.

Your steps	Your spouse's steps
____ 1. Express regret	____ 1. Express regret
____ 2. Accept responsibility	____ 2. Accept responsibility
____ 3. Clarify nonintentionality	____ 3. Clarify nonintentionality
____ 4. Explain the circumstances	____ 4. Explain the circumstances
____ 5. Repair damages	____ 5. Repair damages
____ 6. Learn for the future	____ 6. Learn for the future

As you complete the final step, learning for the future, answer the following questions. What might you each as individuals do differently in the future to prevent a repeat? What as a couple can you restructure so that similar upsets will not occur?

Prevent Affairs, Addictions, and Abuse

For the big three out-of-bounds marriage mistakes—affairs, addictions, and abusive anger—an ounce of prevention is worth way more than a pound of cure. Unfortunately, all-too-many marriages hit difficult tumult because these foreseeable problems were not anticipated, or because someone who knew that what they were doing might create problems didn't listen to quiet internal warning voices.

Naivete—a lack of full understanding of what is safe and what invites indiscretions or excesses in these areas—can be dangerous. Naivete can result in devasting bouts of infidelity, destructive alcohol and drug use, and abusive anger. Serious thinking ahead about how you will avoid these traps is highly worthwhile. Note that you are at increased risk for any of these three difficulties if you know very little about them, or if you have one or more parents who indulged in them.

Big problems start with small slippages. The concept of the slippery slope is important here. Most major mistakes start with small steps that appear to be taken where the terrain seems neither slippery nor sloped. But a few step further on the slope steepens. By then, stopping and turning back are for more difficult.

"I can handle this" is an especially dangerous guide to follow in these areas. If you ever have that thought, you will almost always be thankful later if you translate the thought to mean, "This is inviting trouble."

Most people do foresee danger ahead as they begin affairs, additions, or abusive anger. The problem is that they ignore the danger signs and dismiss the warning thoughts. Beware!

Affairs

Most infidelities start with minor infractions like flirtatious interactions when your spouse is not in sight. Be especially wary of drinking and socializing on business trips or engaging in personal talk alone in private places with a neighbor, business associate, or old friend.

To damage a marriage, an affair does not require sexual intercourse or sexual contact of any sort. Emotional affairs such as e-mail romances or excessive intimacy with work colleagues siphon off to someone else affections that would otherwise go to your partner. Emotional affairs are infidelities. They violate emotional monogamy. And they often lead to physical betrayals as well.

To prevent infidelities, follow these two rules:

The basic rule of marital fidelity: If you would not act in this way with your spouse next to you watching, do not do it. If you are doing anything in any relationship that feels secret, you need to take a second look.

The open-door rule for prevention of infidelities: Keep an open door when meeting with a member of the opposite sex. Stay away from situations in which you would be alone with a person of the opposite sex unless you would be alone for strictly professional reasons and talking only about business. Any violations of this rule put you at risk.

To avoid problems with affairs, think carefully and honestly about the following.

- Are you involved in any flirtations or intimate interactions that would be uncomfortable or upsetting for your spouse to see?

- Do you talk about your personal life with anyone of the opposite sex other than your spouse?

- Did either of your parents ever find themselves involved in betrayal behavior? If so, find out all you can about their experience. As the saying goes, we are destined to repeat history if we do not understand it.

Emotional and sexual faithfulness to your spouse leaves no room for a second partner of any sort. The bottom line is that affairs undermine the basic trust between the two of you that you will be always number one for each other. Commitment and loyalty to one another form the foundation stones for a loving marriage partnership. When these stones are removed by relationship betrayals, the marriage becomes shaky and dissolution can loom as a major threat.

Addictions

Addictions also ruin marriages. Whether addictions are to drugs, alcohol, TV sports, gambling, golf, work, or an eating disorder, addictive habits place the relationship between you and the addictive habit above the relationship between you and your spouse. In this regard, addictions are similar to affairs.

At the same time, addictions generally also bring with them unacceptable interactions with your spouse. Drugs and alcohol, for instance, will tend to lead you to behave in a way that is different from and less attractive than the you whom your spouse chose to marry. Whether addictive substances make you passive or aggressive, talkative or silent, silly or absent, the change is likely to be for the worse in your spouse's eyes.

Take a serious look at your alcohol consumption and an equally or more serious look at any other drugs you may be using. Look also at excesses in other areas of your life. Be honest with yourself. Almost all people who have genuine addictions minimize the negative impacts the addiction is having in their life.

To avoid addictions, think carefully and honestly about the following.

- Does your use of alcohol or another excessive habit have any negative impact whatsoever on your marriage or on your job functioning?

- Has your spouse ever complained about your use of alcohol or other excesses?

- Does the alcohol you drink or other addictive habits ever tempt you to other indiscretions such as affairs or excessive anger?

- Did either of your parents ever drink too much?

- Did either of your parents use other addictive substances or have other addictive habits?

If you answered yes, or even maybe, to any of these questions, talk with your spouse about the problem and consider seeking professional help.

Abusive Anger

Excessive anger is anger that is unpleasant to live with. Abusive anger is anger, expressed verbally or with physical aggression, that is emotionally or physically harmful. If you have an abuse problem or are a spouse of someone who becomes abusively angry, take action immediately. Call your local abuse hot line. Get professional help and, if the situation is imminently dangerous, leave. Go stay with friends or relatives or at a safe house.

Excessive anger is intended to coerce a spouse into doing what the spouse does not want to do, and often stems from emotional hypersensitivity.

Abusive anger establishes a relationship of power over the spouse. Abusive anger usually begins with verbal insults and criticism and may develop into pushing and shoving, hitting, and worse. Abusive anger usually occurs in cycles. Periods of outburst alternate with periods of calm followed by a gradual building of tensions toward the next abusive episode. Abusive battering episodes may be unrelated to apparent household disagreements, except in the mind of the abuser.

In general, spouses whose anger becomes abusive tend to also be controlling, that is, they make rampant crossovers. They frequently tell their spouse what to do and tend to become preoccupied what they think their spouse thinks, feels, or should do.

The dangerousness of abuse is significantly increased with alcohol or drugs. Most serious injuries from abuse occur when the abuser has been drinking. Significant emotional stresses such as job losses and family illnesses can also put someone with an anger problem at higher risk for causing serious injury to loved ones.

Men and women with excessive or abusive anger often find it hard to see that they have an anger problem. Partly this difficulty occurs because that justify their anger by blaming the person they are mad at: "I only got mad like that because s/he . . ." This kind of difficulty taking responsibility suggests a heightened likelihood that the anger is excessive or abusive.

To self-diagnose problems with anger, think carefully and honestly about the following:

- Do you feel you have to get mad to get your spouse to do what you want?

- Do you often become angry? More than once in a blue moon?

- Do you often become intensely angry as opposed to a bit irritated?

- Do you say mean words? Call your spouse names?

- Do you threaten to injure your spouse if what bothers you continues?

- Do you sometimes get so mad that you throw or punch things?

- Do you sometimes get so mad that you push, shake, or strike your spouse?

- Did either of your parents have frequent or intense anger outbursts, verbal or physical, against the other parent, you, or your siblings?

- Was there sexual abuse of any kind in your family?

If you answered yes to even one of the questions above, it is vitally important that you do some thorough rethinking. Talk these issues over with your spouse. Investigate options for anger groups, or talk with religious leaders or mental health professionals whom you trust.

Earlier in this chapter you learned the importance of not threatening divorce. There is a caveat to this rule. The three behaviors you just read about—affairs, addictions, and abuse—can all be grounds for ending a marriage.

Diane Medved and Dan Quayle, co-authors of the 1993 book *The Case Against Divorce*, are strongly pro-marriage. They nonetheless point out that affairs, addictions, and abusive anger, plus danger to self or others, untreatable mental illness or unwillingness to get treatment, dishonesty, gross irresponsibility, or criminal activity are legitimate deal breakers. Often it can be difficult for a spouse to admit that a partner has these serious problems. If in thinking about your spouse, you have even subtle concerns that one of these situations may exist, consider seeking help to determine the best course of action.

Beware of Making Things Worse

Totally out-of-bounds behaviors such as infidelities, addictions, and excessive anger can be difficult to admit to. Rather than feel the embarrassment, shame, and guilt that might arise with admitting that you have these problems, you may be tempted to try to hide the difficulties.

Four strategies for hiding from admitting to out-of-bounds behavior are particularly common yet almost always make the situation worse:

Blame the victim: "It's your fault. I only did it because you . . ."

Blame the messenger: "You have no right to spy on me. You shouldn't have snooped!"

Denial: "No I didn't . . ." "I don't have a problem with . . ." "You're wrong."

Minimize: "Everyone drinks." "I'm not having an affair. It's just a friendship." "I just get a little hot under the collar; that's normal."

Hone Your Skills

Identify which of the four ways of hiding listed above Wanda and Drew use in the following examples. Some of the examples illustrate more than one hiding strategy.

1. Drew: I can't believe you were batting your eyes at him so blatantly. I felt betrayed.

Wanda: What were you doing showing up at my office? That's my territory!

How is Wanda hiding? _____

2. Wanda: (recoils while Drew slams his fist into the wall) Uh, Drew . . .

Drew: *(screams)* Now listen, I don't have an anger problem. I'm just really mad. It's normal for guys to blow off steam. You're the one with the problem. You're always complaining.

How is Drew hiding? _____

3. Drew: I'm getting worried that you've been drinking again.

Wanda: Well, it's your fault. You leave me alone all the time, and you always keep the liquor cabinet full. And you don't understand how stressed I am. You'd drink too!

How is Wanda hiding? _____

4. Wanda: Drew, someone just hung up again after I answered the phone.

Drew: You're making a big deal out of nothing. It's all in your imagination.

How is Drew hiding? _____

The bottom line is that avoiding acknowledgment of your problems will probably result in their getting worse. Blaming the victim, blaming the messenger, denying problems, and minimizing continue the damage to both of you and to your marriage. Instead of allowing your problems to worsen over time, talk them over openly with your spouse and consider getting help.

Summing Up and Moving On

Whenever you experience an upsetting moment, small or large, you can put the puzzle pieces together, identify the misses, and create a full apology. Be especially sure that you conclude by converting your curses to blessings with learning for the future. Mistakes are for learning.

As we have said already several times, if these cleanup procedures alone do not detoxify damaging incidents and do not prevent a recurrence of similar upsets, consider consulting a professional. Most couples wait far too long—seven years on the average!—before they get counseling help. A little bit of help early on, by contrast, can nip problems in the bud.

Cleaning up after upsets is usually like washing cuts and adding a bandage for safe healing. After major incidents, by contrast, cleaning up may be more like setting broken bones. For more severely damaging problems like affairs, addictions, and excessive or abusive anger, you are well advised to get professional help immediately.

Time now to move on to the fun parts of marriage—how to support each other effectively, how to enhance your intimacy, and how to be sure that your marriage is brimming over with affection and enjoyment.

CHAPTER 11

Supporting Your Spouse

Research has confirmed that marriage is a very good deal for most people. According to researcher Linda Waite and journalist Maggie Gallagher, in their outstanding book, *The Case for Marriage* (2000), married people on the whole feel a greater sense of well-being and experience more successes in their lives than people who are single. Marriages with a lot of fighting may lose the benefits. But most married couples do better at their jobs, earn more money, participate in more frequent sex, enjoy sex more, and maintain better emotional and physical health than their unmarried peers of the same education and income levels. Happily married people in general even live longer and have happier children than their single or unhappily married peers.

Why does a good marriage confer so many blessings?

One explanation is that with two people dividing up the labor of living, each is less likely to become overloaded. Two can share the many tasks involved in the business of living. A second set of eyes can watch the stock market while you are envisioning how to redo the living room this year to brighten it up. A second set of arms can lug in groceries while you fix a quick but tasty dinner. A second set of hands can diaper a baby while you repair a faucet leak.

Another explanation for why a good marriage seems to bring so many blessings may be that two heads genuinely can be better than one. A backup brain can find your lost keys, remind you to call Aunt Jennie on her birthday, and validate your intuition that it's time to ask for a raise.

A third explanation, and the one that is explored in the exercises of this chapter, is that marriage gives each spouse a personal live-in therapist. When problems in living arise, as they do from time to time in everyone's life, a married person can turn to this in-house counselor to talk over the dilemma.

What Helps?

Clarity about what kinds of reactions to your spouse's moments of distress are likely to prove positive and which responses to avoid can further ensure that when your spouse needs your support, you can be helpful.

Hone Your Skills

In the first column of the following lists, check the responses that you think would be helpful. Then look at the second column. Check those that you sometimes have used, for better or for worse.

What you think would be helpful	Those you have said or done
____ Reach out with a hug.	____ Reached out with a hug.
____ Ask what's wrong.	____ Asked what's wrong.
____ Listen with concern.	____ Listened with concern.
____ Say, "Don't worry."	____ Said, "Don't worry."
____ Say, "Don't make such a big deal about it."	____ Said, "Don't make such a big deal about it."
____ Say, "Get over it!"	____ Said, "Get over it!"
____ Say, "You shouldn't have have _____," pointing out what your spouse should should have done differently.	____ Said, "You shouldn't have _____," pointing out what your spouse should have done differently.
____ Feel annoyed by your spouse's upset feelings.	____ Felt annoyed by your spouse's upset feelings.
____ Say, "You need to _____," implying that if your spouse what would do what you say, he or she would be fine.	____ Said, "You need to _____," implying that if your spouse would do what you say, he or she would be fine.

The first three responses in the lists above clearly convey support. The remaining responses range from iffy to distinctly unhelpful.

The line between helpful and unhelpful reassurance can be fuzzy. Positive messages of reassurance packaged in I-statements, like "I'm confident that," will tend to be helpful.

A big hug accompanied by a heartfelt "don't worry" can be reassuring. For the most part, however, telling someone not to worry is like telling them not to feel what they feel, or not to regard feelings as trustworthy. Negating feelings seldom is helpful. *And* messages are preferable, "I can understand your anxiety about the talk you have to give, *and* . . ."

If you say, "don't worry" with a critical tone in your voice, your words surely will have a distressing impact. Minimizing the problem—"It's not so bad"— is also likely to be unhelpful unless you can add specific encouraging information that explains why the problem is less serious than it may have seemed. Criticism of any sort is likely to feel undermining rather than supportive.

The last option on the chart above, offering solutions, may or may not prove helpful. Asking your spouse what options might be possible can be constructive, but thinking up solutions to your spouse's problem, while well-intentioned, risks being heard as a cross-over. Worse, insisting that your spouse do what you think is a good solution will invite tensions between you, adding a power struggle to the already existing difficulties.

On the other hand, telling your spouse what to do can sometimes be helpful and in emergencies can even be essential. A new solution idea can trigger new thinking even if that particular idea won't work. If your spouse can think of no further solution options, your ideas may break the logjam. In emergencies, like when a truck is coming as you cross the street, grabbing your spouse's arm makes sense.

In general, however, the foundation skills for helpfulness are the listening skills for hearing feelings that you learned early on in this workbook.

Listen to Feelings: A Review for Offering Support

The basic listening principles that you learned in chapter 4 and reviewed in chapter 7 for listening effectively when your spouse is angry, are key to supporting your spouse in other emotionally difficult times.

- Feelings first: If you see a frown, a moist tear, or a twinkling eye, ask about these before continuing on.

- Ask open-ended *how* and *what* questions to clarify the feelings and the problem bringing on these feelings.

- Listen to learn: Listen to understand, not to criticize.

- Avoid negating with *but*.

- Digest aloud what you hear, so your spouse knows what you are taking in.

- Respond with *yes, and*. After digesting aloud what makes sense to you about what was said, add your perspective with *and*.

Hone Your Skills

Imagine yourself in the following situation. Create helpful responses that use the skills you have learned. Use your imagination to fill in what you and your spouse might say.

Hint: You are trying to understand more about your spouse's concerns. You do not need to create a solution.

Your spouse sighs, saying "I'm so discouraged."

You: _____

_____

Your spouse: _____

_____

You: _____

_____

Your spouse: _____

_____

You: _____

_____

Your spouse: _____

_____

Checklist: Did you

____ respond to feelings first?

____ use *how* or *what* questions to ask for more information?

____ listen to learn?

____ digest aloud what your spouse said to you?

____ use *yes, and* to add information that could be helpful?

With these listening guidelines to rely on, when your spouse looks sad, stressed, or in need of support, you can pause and mentally test-drive your response before you voice it.

In some cases, however, your spouse may confront a dilemma that seems to need more than brief concerned listening. Counselor-like skills such as those taught to therapists in *From Conflict to Resolution* (Heitler 1994) can be helpful for these more challenging times. These skills are an expanded version of the listening and win-win problem-solving you have been learning. The baseball metaphor below explains how to use these skills to facilitate your spouse's feeling better.

Be a Super Supporter

To support your distressed spouse, you can think of yourself as a baseball coach. The steps you take follow the same sequence as those you take in the win-win waltz, but note that a waltz is a dance you do together. You work together symmetrically to accomplish conflict resolution and shared problem-solving. To help your spouse through difficult situations, by contrast, the role of the helper is more like a coach. The player does the base running; the coach just asks guiding questions.

Solving a problem actually has much in common with scoring a run in baseball. Both require touching all the bases. Reaching solutions, like scoring a run, feels great.

Each base in this game represents a different set of questions. As coach, you prepare the runner at each base to move on to the next by asking the key questions of that stage of the problem-solving process.

The essential point to remember is that your spouse is the batter and must do the running from base to base. Your job is not to solve the problem but to serve as a coach by asking good questions.

Play Ball!

The diagram below shows a batter at home plate plus the three bases that need touching in order to score a run, a solution to the problem.

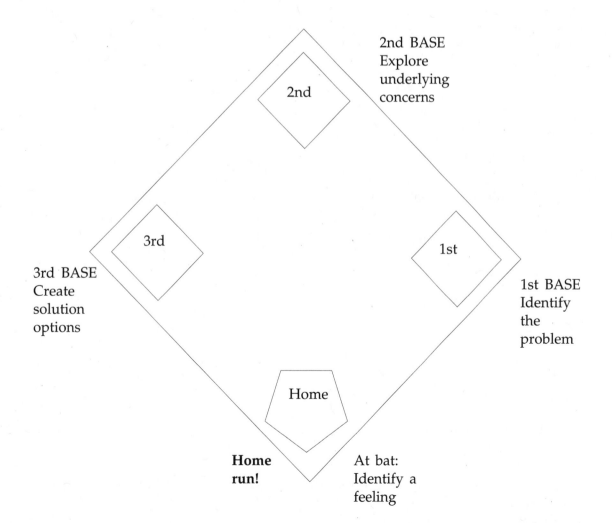

2nd BASE
Explore
underlying
concerns

3rd BASE
Create
solution
options

1st BASE
Identify
the
problem

Home run!

At bat:
Identify a
feeling

Support Your Spouse the Baseball Way

Base	Batter's Task	Coach: Sample Questions
Batting	Identify a negative feeling, e.g., anxiety, hurt, irritation, etc.	I see a frown. How are you feeling? What's up?
1st base	Identify the problem situation	What are you anxious about?
2nd base	Explore the underlying concerns	When did the feeling begin? How did that happen? What do they want? What are your preferences? fears? concerns?
3rd base	Create solution options	What have you thought of doing so far? How else might you handle it?
Home plate	Score a run by choosing a solution	What's the next step you'll take? And after that?

In the following dialogue Raif serves as baseball coach, helping Ruby to work through a problem that has been troubling her.

Ruby looks glum.

Batting: Identify a feeling.

Raif: Ruby, you're looking unusually glum. What's up?

Ruby: You're right. I'm not feeling like my usual peppy self. I feel really down.

1st base: Identify the problem.

Raif: What's on your mind?

Ruby: I can't seem to stop thinking about work. I haven't felt comfortable since that promotion.

Raif: At first it seemed like you were really excited about finally moving up. What's changed?

Ruby: I feel like I'm not doing good work. I constantly feel like I'm letting everyone down.

2nd base: Explore underlying concerns.

Raif: Letting them down? How?

Ruby: Well, I got promoted because my boss saw that I was really good at generating ideas about where the company should go. Now, I seem to be managing a million details. All I do is check if this order went out, or that customer got called, or the technician solved the glitch. I feel like I juggle a hundred balls at once, dropping most of them. It's not what I'm good at.

Raif: I had thought the promotion would free you up for more big-picture work. Sounds like instead it's done the opposite. What else about the change is worrisome?

Ruby: Well, I'm not quite sure. Maybe I'm worried that my boss will begin to wonder if it was a good idea to move me up. Mostly though, I really don't like feeling like I'm constantly dropping balls. I thought this job would be exciting. Instead it's overwhelming.

3rd base: Create solution options.

Raif: Work isn't supposed to be an endurance test. It's so unlike you to feel overwhelmed. And also unlike you to be anything less than 100-percent confident. How could you feel more relaxed?

Ruby: Let's see, I guess one thing I could do is to share my concerns with my boss before she gets annoyed. Maybe she could even hire an administrator to help me keep on top of the details and free me up to do more conceptual work.

Raif: Those sound like great ideas. What other options can you think of?

Ruby: What else could I do? Well, I guess I could try to see this as an opportunity to work on my management skills. I know it wouldn't hurt for me to get better at delegating, even if that will never be my forte.

Score a run: Choose a plan of action.

Raif: Hey, you're smiling again. I feel like the sun just came out.

Ruby: I'm feeling better just thinking about what I could do.

Raif: I'm sure impressed with how quickly you came up with ideas for changing things. You are good at coming up with big-picture solutions! So, which of these ideas are most appealing?

Ruby: I think improving my management skills. There was an e-mail not too long ago about a management training seminar. I didn't pay attention to it then, but now I think it might help. Who knows, with training, I might even come to enjoy this job. Raif, thanks so much for your help. I feel so much better!

Raif succeeded in guiding Ruby to a satisfying resolution of her problem. He commented on her ideas and asked further questions without solving the dilemma for her. He did not try to be Ruby's advisor. Rather, Raif's effectiveness came from his asking a helpful sequence of questions. His questions kept Ruby moving forward from base to base until she arrived at a comprehensive understanding of her problem and picked a plan of action.

Hone Your Skills

Fill in questions that Jason could ask to help Joan solve her problem. Continue until Joan scores a run with a successful solution. After you fill in each of Jason's questions, check if the questions you suggest are effective by reading Joan's answers. Does your question lead to this response?

Joan seemed brittle. At one point she said to Jason, "I'm feeling tense," which was unusual for Joan, who usually is very good-humored and easygoing. Since Joan has identified her feeling, the next step is to help her get to first base.

1st base: Identify the problem situation.

Jason: What _____

Joan: I think I'm anxious about moving to our new house.

2nd base: Explore the underling concerns.

Jason: What _____

Joan: Maybe it's because the new house seems so big.

Jason: Yes, _____

_____

What _____

_____

Joan: Big means that there are so many spaces to fill. I don't know where we'll get enough furniture or how to arrange furniture in that big a space.

Jason: Yes/what else _____

_____

Joan: I guess I'm also worried that we'll feel distant from each other in such a big house. Our little apartment was cramped, but I felt like you and I were close and cozy.

3rd base: Create solution options.

Jason: What/how _____

_____

Joan: I guess maybe I could start with fixing up the first floor. That feels more manageable and less expensive. Alternatively, I could set up the lounge area off the bedroom as a cozy place for us to sit. Or maybe do the kitchen first?

Home plate: Choose a plan of action.

Jason: Those sound like good ideas. What/how _____

_____

Joan: I think maybe I'll start with the lounge. It will be so nice to retreat there if I feel overwhelmed.

Jason: Fabulous. How about I bring up the lounge chairs right now?

Now that you have had an initial experience as base coach, let's explore in additional detail how your coaching can be especially effective.

At Bat

You already know how to help your partner step up to the batting plate: when you notice a feeling, ask about it.

Helpful support starts by taking feelings seriously, using them as keys to open up awareness of a problem. Asking when you see evidence of a feeling launches the ball into play, moving you to first base.

First Base: Identify the Problem

When you see a feeling and want to inquire to identify the situation provoking it, simple questions often work best. One word restating the emotion, with a question mark in your voice, can be plenty: "Sad?" Two-word questions also tend to be fine: "How come?" "What's up?"

The one feeling that takes complicated questioning to clarify is depression. As the audiotape *Depression, A Disorder of Power* explains (Heitler 1994) when depression is hovering, like a dark cloud, the person who is depressed often has no idea why. If your spouse is depressed, you can suggest that your spouse close his or her eyes, allowing an image to come up of who he or she might be mad at. Clarify that *who* other than him/herself, as depression virtually always includes feeling mad at oneself. If you do this exercise, though, be prepared to discover that your spouse is angry at you. The good news is that all data are good data; it's virtually always more helpful to have information, which gives you power to change, than to be clueless.

Hone Your Skills

When Jill and Sam try to help each other feel better in the face of distress, their help is well-intentioned but misguided. Write a brief question that can clarify the triggering problem.

Sam is sitting on the back deck drinking his evening tea with a furrowed brow.

Jill's response: Come on Sam, let's see a little smile. It's a beautiful morning!

A brief question: _____

Jill, trying on a pair of pants that is too small, is sighing.

Sam's response: Jill, stop trying to squeeze into those pants. Just go buy a new pair.

A brief question: _____

Helpful responses take feelings seriously, using them as keys to open up an awareness of a problem.

Second Base: Explore Concerns

Asking *how* and *what* questions about the situation helps your spouse to crystallize what concerns make the situation troubling. For example, "What's going on that you have to work so much longer than usual?" or "How do you feel about the project?"

When, where, and *who* questions can be useful here as well. "When did the extra work load begin?" "Where is the work coming from?" and "Who else is involved?" all can help you to accomplish the project of helping your spouse see the dimensions of the problem more clearly.

How do you know what to ask about? In general, responding to whatever piques your interest will be likely to prove helpful. Stay attuned though. Irritation or resistance from your spouse may be a sign that your questions are getting off track.

Another way to figure out what questions to ask is to note salient words and ask questions that would give you more information about these terms. For instance, your spouse may say, "I get impatient with my boss Quentin because he's so dishonest." Two strong words stand out in this sentence: impatient and dishonest. Your responses could follow up on either, or, better yet, both. "When did you begin feeling impatient like that?" "What do you do when you feel impatient?" "What do you mean by dishonest?" "How did you find out he's dishonest?"

Hone Your Skills

Craft questions to help Sam and Jill explore the concerns underlying each of their dilemmas.

- First, circle the key words that stand out for you in each example.

- Then ask *how, what, when, where,* or *who* questions about each of these words.

Sam: When I look out at the moon, I think I should be feeling peaceful, but instead I feel sad. It makes me think about cemeteries.

Jill's questions:

1. _____

2. _____

3. _____

Jill: I'm so worried. The doctor who gave me my physical said I'm potentially in deep trouble.

Sam's questions:

1. _____

2. _____

3. _____

The main mistakes spouses make on second base are

- cutting the questioning short in a rush to find solutions

- asking too many questions without digesting aloud and adding your viewpoint

- giving too much of your viewpoint

Cutting your questioning short before enough concerns have been clarified is probably the most common mistake helpers make. Racing prematurely on to third base is an especially frequent male error. Unfortunately, skipping second base in a rush to generate solutions is likely to put the batter out; that is, it tends to end the problem solving instead of facilitating it.

Insufficiently exploring concerns can be especially tempting when you think you can see obvious solutions that you are sure would be helpful. Instead of giving in to this temptation, take your time. A few more questions that fully explore your spouse's concerns will yield far better eventual action proposals.

If all you do, however, is ask questions when you try to help, you will begin to come across as an interrogator. React to the answers your spouse gives to your questions by digesting aloud what you hear and adding your thoughts. Just remember that the bulk of the information needs to come from the runner, not from the coach.

Third Base: Generate Solution Options

At third base you may be especially tempted to take over the problem as your own. If you suggest solutions before stimulating your partner to create solution options, however, you may set yourself up for trouble. If the solution works, your spouse will not experience the full satisfaction of having been the creator. If the solution doesn't work, it will be your fault.

Another warning for the coach at third base: Be on the lookout for the word *should.* You learned in chapter 5 how *should* can be a red flag for unnecessary tension and pressure. In addition, *should* is a red flag at third base because *should* blocks creative thinking. The word *could,* by contrast, keeps options open. If your spouse begins to lock in to one option with *should,* leaving no room for additional ideas, try changing the *should* to *could.* When your spouse says, "I should . . . ," try responding with, "Yes, you could."

Should solutions often have a yet another shortcoming. They tend to be dutiful without being fully responsive to all of your spouse's concerns. *Could* may be able to keep your spouse's creative thinking flowing to a more fully satisfying solution. "I should work late tonight." "Yes, you could, and are there other possibilities?" "Well, I could bring the work home, and work at the kitchen table. Actually that would be much nicer, because at least we could be in the same room."

Lastly, remember to seek a solution set. As with the win-win waltz for shared problem-solving, a comprehensive plan with aspects that respond to each of the concerns that have been raised will bring the fullest win-win results.

After you have invited your spouse to come up with solutions, you may still have some ideas that sound to you like good ones. Now, at long last, comes your chance. Here are the principles for adding your ideas:

- Wait to give your ideas until your partner has first had time to devise options.

- Offer your ideas as suggestions, not as *shoulds*.

- Ask what might and might not work about your idea.

- Respect your spouse as the final authority on his or her life, including if he or she decides not to use your ideas.

Home Base: Score a Run

Invite your spouse to choose which plan of actions sounds best. Ask how he or she will get started. Implementing a solution obviously is helpful, but, interestingly, just determining a plan is usually enough to dissipate the negative feeling your spouse started out with.

A word of caution: It sometimes happens that you coach your spouse successfully around the three bases, but no decision is forthcoming. Your spouse seems to be out before reaching home plate. What can the coach do at that point? Offer the tincture of time. "Let's sleep on it and see what thoughts come up tomorrow."

Practice with Your Partner

Identify (each of you) an issue in your life that you would like to be able to think through with help from your spouse. This could be a problem you have been having at work, a dilemma with a friend, a habit you would like to change, or any noncouple dilemma that evokes uncomfortable feelings for you.

Your topic: _____

Your spouse's topic: _____

Now, take turns supporting each other as you attempt to solve these dilemmas. Use the super supporter baseball strategy you have learned in this chapter.

Talk Together

How do you each feel after having had this discussion? What was most helpful about the coaching? How do you feel toward each other after this experience?

Summing Up and Moving On

Spouses feel like best friends when they can turn to each other in hard times. Intimacy coalesces and solidifies when you can talk together about distressing experiences. Spouses also feel like best friends when they share life's joys. Enhancing these joys is the goal of chapter 12.

CHAPTER 12

Intimacy and a Loving Home

At the core of successful marriage partnership lies a mysterious additional phenomenon, the phenomenon we call love. Open communication serves as the lifeblood of a relationship, and skills for dealing with differences keep the relationship from getting stuck, but, like a heart, love must keep throbbing to keep the system alive. Just what is this business of loving?

"I love you." These words often are used to refer to feelings of sexual arousal. The physical feeling of sexual excitement is the aspect of love that most romance focuses upon. Enjoyable sexual feelings are vitally important, and yet are not the full story of love in marriage. The same words, "I love you," also refer to a bonding phenomenon, a development that enables two separate individuals to experience themselves as one couple.

Andras Angyal coined the term *we-feeling* for this aspect of the love phenomenon, that is, for the sense of oneness that couples experience. You are you, and you are a part of a *we*. You and the one you love are separate individuals, each with your own bodies, thoughts, personalities, and preferences. Yet you care as much about your spouse's health, safety, and happiness as about your own, and both of you lovingly protect the *we*.

Caring is the essence of love. When you choose to add marriage to love, you make a decision that of all the people in the world, the one individual that you most care about, and who will most care for you, is your spouse—plus the offspring whom you and your spouse together bring into being.

Caring means listening to your partner's thoughts, feelings, concerns, and comments. Your life is augmented by what your partner experiences. Caring means wanting blessings to come your partner's way as much as in your own direction. Caring means being each other's co-celebrators in times of joy, cheerleaders in times of challenge, and supporters in times of disappointment and difficulty. If you are preoccupied with your own life to the extent that you are unable to focus on what your spouse is experiencing, you are not engaged in loving. You may in the abstract love your spouse, and enjoy much sexual pleasure together, but to be loving in a relationship requires activity and attitudes that are loving.

In addition to caring, loving involves a particular kind of seeing. Love is seeing with appreciation. Love is not blind. Love is seeing in a very special light, in the best possible light. Love may involve seeing problems, but problems viewed in a loving light evoke compassion, not judgment; love triggers problem solving, not criticism.

A woman grieving the loss of her husband in an accident once summed up well what it is to love. In her sadness she realized with sudden clarity, "I forgot to cherish him!" Continuing, she realized, "I seldom appreciated all he did. I didn't tell him often enough how much I enjoyed his companionship, his humor, his deeply furrowed brow when he thought. I never even realized myself how much I valued the financial stability and the always-there-for-me steadiness he brought to my life. I forgot to cherish him!"

This chapter is a series of reminders to cherish your loved one, and suggestions on how to do so.

Intimacy

Marriage is a safe harbor for intimacy. Most people would agree that intimacy is one of the unique and extraordinary benefits of marriage, but what is this elusive and yet quintessential aspect of a loving marriage?

The term *intimacy* is derived from a Latin word, *intimus*, which means innermost. *Innermost* itself is an interesting word, as it means the superlative, or strongest form of, *interior*. That is, intimacy involves sharing the most interior parts of yourself—your most personal and private thoughts, emotions, and physical parts. Intimacy involves an intertwining of the most internally primary parts of your lives—how and when and where you eat, sleep, pray, conceive and raise your children, plan for your future, and more.

Time fosters intimacy. Sharing of your most private aspects of being occurs gradually over time. Time refers to how much time you devote to sharing together, and to how long you have known each other. Length of association gives you a sense of "knowing" each other in the sense of familiarity with each other's habits, facial expressions, preferences, values, and other attributes. In successful marriages, marriages in which communication flows comfortably, the sense of intimate connection, of your lives being deeply intertwined and of knowing each other sexually and emotionally, grows over time.

Intimacy Takes Time

How can intimacy be enhanced? Intimacy builds with time together. Both the quantity and the quality of time you enjoy as a couple play major roles in how closely connected you feel.

Newlyweds tend to do well at reserving time to share with each other. As children arrive, and as work responsibilities enlarge, spouses can drift into separate worlds. Especially when work takes up more than eight hours a day, or if children's bedtimes are late, reserving time for the marriage relationship can prove to be a major challenge. You may need to make a conscious choice to cordon off specific time together in order to adequately nurture your couplehood.

Hone Your Skills

How well are you able to fit it all in? Assess your time allotments:

_____ My work hours give me enough time at work and enough time at home.

_____ I reserve some time for exercise and for my individual interests.

_____ (if applicable) I arrange time alone each day with each of my children.

_____ We enjoy daily time together as a full family. Mealtimes especially.

_____ We share at least some time together as a couple every day, with additional time on weekends.

Setting aside enough couple time, including enough time alone together, can help to keep your sense of togetherness, the power of your two-ness, solid.

You can prevent inadvertent distancing by periodically reassessing your together time. The chart below can help you. When you do something unusual or something particularly satisfying together, your connection will feel especially refreshed. At the same time, seeing each other contributing to the work of family life—from taking out the garbage to arranging flowers on the window sill—replenishes and augments your sense of satisfaction in being a couple. In addition, doing ordinary day-to-day activities together, like cleaning the kitchen, child care, paying the bills, watching a football game, or sitting on the couch sharing what has gone on that day, all enhance your sense of partnership. As you do these activities, the more you openly communicate your thoughts and feelings, following the talking and listening guidelines you have learned for smooth and safe information flow, the more intimate your partnership will feel.

Looking back over the past week, use the chart on the following page to clarify for yourself how you divided your nonwork hours. Calculate first how many awake hours you have left once you have subtracted those hours you devote to work. Then divide this daily number of nonwork hours into three categories: those you spend alone, with others (who may or may not include your spouse), and with your spouse alone. Do the times in each category seem sufficient?

Day	Total nonwork hours	Nonwork hours not with your spouse	Nonwork hours with your spouse plus others (i.e., children, friends)	Nonwork hours together alone as a couple
Monday				
Tuesday				
Wednesday				
Thursday				
Friday				
Saturday				
Sunday				

Talk Together

Share your chart with your spouse. How do each of you feel about your time distribution? How might you alter your schedule to improve your time allotments?

Carving out ample time for working together, talking, fun, and sex keeps your couplehood intimate, vigorous, and invigorating.

"We" Matters

Earlier in this book, we looked at how couples sometimes use the word *we* in a way that is problematic, that is, when *we* is really an *I* or a *you*. At the same time, there are times when the word *we* captures your important sense of partnership. Often, when couples feel most like a team, a *we* in the best sense, it comes from doing activities together.

Practice with Your Partner

The following chart suggests various arenas in which couples enjoy time together. Which do you, or might you, enjoy?

Activity realms	What we like to do together	What we might do more
Sports and games		
Religious/spiritual		
Entertainment		
Child-related		
Art, music, or dance		
Television		
Socializing		
Political activity		
Community		
Housekeeping		
Home improvement		
Yard and garden		
Hobbies		
Cooking		
Volunteer work		
Exercise		
Nature		
Sex		
Relaxation		
Other		

Talk Together

Discuss the activities you each enjoy doing with the other. What else might you do in the coming weeks to enhance your sense of togetherness?

Trust Invites Intimacy

Intimacy flourishes where openness is safe. Each of you has the power to make your home safe for sharing vulnerable thoughts and sensitive feelings—and also the power to create an unsafe environment. Where there is safety, there is trust. Where there is no safety, there is no trust, and intimacy is ill-advised.

Hone Your Skills

Rate yourself from 1 (not so well) to 5 (extremely well) on how well you build trust in each of the following areas.

Trustworthy behavior	How do you do?
I generally respond with interest, not criticism, when my spouse shares his or her thoughts and feelings.	1 2 3 4 5
I talk about my concerns in a tactful way instead of becoming critical.	1 2 3 4 5
I follow up by doing what I have said I will do.	1 2 3 4 5
I am reliable about being on time when we meet.	1 2 3 4 5
I am tactful when I say what I feel.	1 2 3 4 5
I am slow to anger and quick to cool down.	1 2 3 4 5
I contribute my fair share to the work of sustaining our family.	1 2 3 4 5
I am there for my spouse when he or she needs me.	1 2 3 4 5
I keep confidential things that my spouse tells me are private.	1 2 3 4 5
I make no negative comments about my spouse to others.	1 2 3 4 5
I check with my spouse before making large purchases.	1 2 3 4 5
I consult with my spouse on matters in my own life that may impact him or her.	1 2 3 4 5

I am loyal, standing up for my spouse when he or she is threatened in any way.	1 2 3 4 5
I am faithful sexually.	1 2 3 4 5
I am faithful emotionally, avoiding overly personal conversations with others that would feel inappropriate to him or her.	1 2 3 4 5
I try to be responsive to what my spouse wants.	1 2 3 4 5
I share my concerns and feelings with my spouse so he or she can understand me deeply.	1 2 3 4 5
I talk with my spouse when we have different views so that eventually we come to a consensus on issues that might otherwise divide us.	1 2 3 4 5
I care deeply for my spouse's well-being.	1 2 3 4 5

Talk Together

Look over your responses, and share your thoughts on these with your spouse. Be sure you each evaluate yourselves. In addition, sharing what you appreciate in your spouse is helpful. Requesting what you would like more of can also lead to fruitful—though sensitive—discussion.

- What are you pleased about in your trustworthiness?

- Which does your spouse feel he or she does well?

- What can each of you do to make your home feel more safe, and your actions feel more trustworthy?

Sexual Intimacy

How seriously do you regard the role of sex in your relationship? Good sex does not guarantee a good marriage, but inadequate or infrequent sexual intercourse makes a marriage more likely to develop problems. Mutual enjoyment of sexual activity is generally a vital ingredient of a good marriage.

How does sex contribute to a strong and loving marriage? First, sex is good for your physical bodies. At the least, it's a good workout; better yet, like a good night's sleep, sex seems to help to keep bodies well tuned. Sexual activity and release also keep emotional systems humming along with optimized energy and relaxation. Good sex often yields good moods.

Sex is definitely a positive way to pass time together. Like dancing or playing music, sexual activity can be an exhilarating arena for creativity, beauty, and spirituality. Couples typically develop standard simple sex routines, augmented by special times in which they discover new choreography, even after forty years of marriage. A wide range of sexual experiences is common in couples who enjoy a fell sexual life together. Some encounters are quickies, maybe more for him or her than for both; other encounters are more fully exciting and more likely to invite elaborate inventiveness.

No need to wait for a romantic vacation. No need to wait for good weather. Sex can be available day and night, wind, sun, or rain. It's fun and it's free. A very good deal!

Hone Your Skills

To ensure that you maintain a full and positive sexual relationship, consider the following sexual-connecting checklist. Rate how accurately each of the following sentences describes you. Use a scale of 1 to 5, in which 1 means rarely and 5 means always. The higher the score, the healthier your sex life is likely to be.

Sexual Sharing	How do you do? 1 = very little 5 = a lot
I enjoy our sexual time together.	1 2 3 4 5
I make intimate time a priority if we have gone longer than usual without sexual time together.	1 2 3 4 5
I prepare for sexual time, bathing and beautifying.	1 2 3 4 5
I make it a point to look attractive at home, especially in the evenings.	1 2 3 4 5
I am careful to say only positive comments about my spouse's body.	1 2 3 4 5
I share responsibility for initiating sexual time.	1 2 3 4 5
I listen to my spouse's desires.	1 2 3 4 5
I find ways to keep our sexual activity fresh and gratifying.	1 2 3 4 5
I notice and comment when my spouse looks especially attractive.	1 2 3 4 5
I find ways to go to bed before I am too exhausted for sexual time together.	1 2 3 4 5
I indicate to my partner what I find satisfying.	1 2 3 4 5
I am receptive to my partner's sexual advances.	1 2 3 4 5

Most communication about sex is nonverbal, through sounds, touch, and body movement. The basics you have learned for verbal communication apply to nonverbal sexual communicating as well.

What can you do during sexual activities that would be equivalent to talking with tact?

_____

_____

_____

What can you do during sexual activities that would be equivalent to listening to learn?

_____

_____

_____

What can you do during sexual activities that would be equivalent to sustaining collaborative dialogue? _____

_____

_____

Keeping Your House a Loving Home

This workbook has been about becoming the kind of spouse and the kind of couple for whom living happily ever after can be a reality. No one can guarantee health, wealth, a meaningful career, or the blessing of fertility, but you can control how you will deal as a couple with the blessings and disappointments that head your way.

The remaining pages of this book offer some other arenas to consider in creating the home life you genuinely would like for your life and your marriage.

Division of Labor Makes Labor More Loving

Interdependence contributes to a positive sense of couplehood, to a positive sense of togetherness. When you rely on your spouse and your spouse relies on you, the two of you together are enjoying the benefits of the power of two.

Lack of clarity about who handles which household responsibilities, however, can generate unfortunate tensions. Housework then goes undone or gets duplicated. Vagueness invites squabbles about who is doing what to keep the household going. Division of labor vagueness can also make the distribution appear unfair, causing resentments.

- For the second week in a row, neither of you take out the trash.

- You bounce a check because you think your spouse is responsible for keeping adequate funds in your joint checking account.

- You feel you deserve to be free of household chores since you bring home the paycheck, but your spouse keeps asking you to help.

Clarity about who does what is helpful. By contrast, blurring this clarity by too frequently helping or asking each other for help can be surprisingly provocative.

Willingness to help expresses caring and love, so how can too much helping be a problem? When your spouse is carrying too many grocery bags and you reach out a helping hand, you probably generate a mutual spurt of loving feelings. However, if helping becomes hovering, it can feel choking. If helping becomes insisting that the other does activities in your way, because your way will be better, the helping becomes controlling. Giving each other space to be separate people and yet being there when help really matters are dual goals, both worth aiming for.

How about asking for help? "Could you please help me to move the stove so I can clean behind it?" The task goes beyond what you can do alone. The power of two is necessary to accomplish it. "Would you pass me the salt please?" makes sense if you are far from the salt and your spouse is near it. And asking is clearly preferable to expecting your spouse on mind-read when you need help.

On the other hand, "Will you put the laundry in the washer for me while I run to the store for milk?" can be problematic. It assumes that what is on your plate is more important than what your spouse was doing. Asking for help with your own agenda subtracts from whatever your spouse had planned to do with that time. The assumption here is that your spouse has nothing to do but to comply with your requests. Frequent requests, therefore, suggest disrespect for your partner's uses of his or her energies. This stance is likely to provoke irritation.

Clear division of labor solves the problem of excessive helping. Working together in collaboration, rather than depending on helping each other, breeds love. You could agree, for instance, that washing clothes is your job, folding is a together activity, and putting the clean clothes away is your spouse's domain. Clear definition of who will do what predicts smooth teamwork—"I'll set the table." "Great, and I'll do the food, and if the salad isn't ready in time, I'd love a co-worker." "Perfect."

Practice with Your Partner

If you and your spouse have vagueness about division of labor and resulting tensions about who is responsible for what, then it's time for you to talk. The following system for divvying up responsibilities can keep your home humming smoothly.

- Create a list of what needs doing.
- Mark on the list what each of you is willing to volunteer for.
- Decide who does the rest—divvy up the other jobs or hire others to do them.
- Double-check that the system is working by discussing it over the coming days.
- Reallocate pieces until the plan feels just right.
- Notice when your spouse finishes a task. Express your appreciation.
- Speak up and say it when the division of labor needs more fix-it talk.

The following chart delineating household chores can help you to clarify who does what in your home. Note tasks like washing dishes that lend themselves to doing jointly for more *we*-time.

General area	Specific tasks	Who does each task?
Cleaning		
Finances		
Food		
Maintenance/repairs		
Children		
Social life		
Other		

A household is like a business—a family is a unit that together accomplishes the business of living. Like a business, a family runs most happily with clear delegation of responsibilities.

Let the Sun Shine

Just like a garden blossoms when the weather is sunny, marriages flower under emotional sunshine. Appreciation and affection are sunshine for intimate partners. A marriage feels all the more bountiful as goodwill and warmth increase.

Practice with Your Partner

Over the next week track the frequency and ways that you and your spouse express warmth in your marriage. Once a day, put a check mark for whatever ways you emanated or received sunshine that day. The goal is to accumulate multiple check marks in each box for each spouse.

Way of expressing sunshine	You did this	Your spouse did this
Initiate a hug, a snuggle, or a gentle touch.		
Agree with something your spouse has said.		
Pitch in and help with something you don't usually do in the household.		
Gladly do your part of the household functioning.		
Express admiration (e.g., "I like that color on you").		
Express thanks for something your spouse has done.		
Smile.		
Be playful.		
Declare your love.		
Initiate sexual time.		
Focus on pleasuring your partner.		
Talking together, say what you appreciate.		
Discuss a personal dilemma.		

Share about your day, discussing issues on your mind.		
Set aside time to hang out together.		
Do an activity together you both enjoy.		
Together, help someone or do a volunteer project.		
Inquire about something of importance to your spouse.		
Give a gift—something you make or find or buy.		
Laugh together		
Cherish your spouse		

Summing Up and the Big Picture

This last chapter, on intimacy and a loving home, hopefully has stimulated your thinking about how to maximize the positives in your marriage. A marriage rich in closeness and affection thrives from setting aside private couple time for talking over the details of your separate and shared lives. A marriage is further enriched when you share upkeep of day-to-day tasks, as well when you enjoy communal, religious, athletic, artistic, and other leisure activities together. Of all activities you share, sexual time may be the most important for keeping your relationship continually revitalized.

The environment that makes intimacy safe is based on trust. Trust is multifaceted—confidence that there will be no sexual betrayals, clarity that you will protect and defend each other, and commitment that you will take care not to hurt each other.

Freud, the father of modern psychological thinking, used to say that a healthy individual is one who can work and love. A healthy family does the same. A division of labor in your home that feels clear and fair, and yet flexible in response to changing circumstances, provides the basis for a smoothly running family life. In addition, in a marriage that resonates with love, sunshine from the shared affection and attentiveness, keeps the climate comfortable bright and warm.

This brings us to graduation time! Congratulations for having completed this workbook, which took many hours of focused attention from you.

At the same time, the work of building a strong and loving relationship clearly is not over. That project is lifelong. Change happens over time. A good sports coach knows that between teaching players new techniques and seeing the players able to use the techniques in games there is a time lag. First the player can perform the new skill occasionally with the coach, and then more consistently. Even then, however, there almost always is a period of consolidation before the player can rely consistently on the new technique in tournament play. Be patient with yourself and your spouse. Appreciate the gains you both are making. Stay with the learning process until the new skills have become integrated into your repertoire to the point that they are automatic in even the most sensitive of moments.

In the introduction we suggested that you save your completed workbook and refer back to it over the coming years. If technical glitches seem to be undermining your goodwill when the two of you talk together, review the pages on talking, listening, and dialogue to recall which of the many details that sustain skillful cooperative flow need reconsolidating. If anger is tainting your time together, remember that anger is a stop sign, and review how to stop, look, and listen. Flip straight to the specific chapter you need when an upsetting event needs healing, when a repeatedly frustrating situation needs fix-it talk, or when you feel stymied in the face of a difficult decision ahead.

This book has aimed to be practical. Before ending, however, let's take a few moments to wax philosophical. How does learning marriage communication skills fit into the big picture of good and evil in the world? Evil has been described as anything that hurts or smothers life (Peck, 1997). Goodness, by contrast, is whatever promotes life's positives—love, smiles, creative endeavors, healing, appreciation, productive activity, hugs, joy.

Each person, every day, at every moment, can choose to insult, criticize, complain, or otherwise indulge in negativity. While such negativity may not quite qualify as full evil, it certainly heads in that direction. By contrast, every person, every day, at every moment, can choose a path of goodness. Goodness is the path where you say directly what you would like, where you respect and verbalize feelings, where you listen to learn, digest appreciatively what makes sense to you in what you hear, and braid your dialogue by adding thoughts. Goodness is where anger is a stop sign that points out difficulties and leads to fixing, not force-it talk. Goodness is where you discover creative solutions that join you together with the dialogue dance of the win-win waltz. Goodness is where you heal by putting together the big picture and using apologies to learn and grow. Goodness is supporting each other and enjoying intimate times together.

All over the world, whenever two people, two companies, or even two countries interact, the potential emerges for a harming moment or for a positive and creative moment that enriches the lives of both. Choose to enrich your life. This is the power of two. As the songwriter Emily Saliers puts it, multiply life by the power of two.

References

Angyal, A. 1965. *Neurosis and Treatment: A Holistic Theory*. New York: Wiley.

Fisher, R., and W. Ury. 1981. *Getting to Yes*. New York: Penguin Books

Gottman, J. M., and N. Silver. 2000. *The Seven Principles for Making Marriage Work*. New York: Three Rivers Press (Crown).

Heitler, S. 1994. *From Conflict to Resolution*. New York: Norton.

Heitler, S. 1994. *Depression, A Disorder of Power*. (audio tape) Denver: TherapyHelp.com.

Medved, D., and D. Quayle. 1993. *The Case against Divorce*. New York: Ivy Books.

Peck, M. S. 1997. *The People of the Lie: The Hope for Healing Human Evil*. 2nd edition. New York: Touchstone Books.

Tannen, D. 1990. *You Just Don't Understand*. New York: Ballantine Books.

Waite, L. J., and M. Gallagher. 2000. *The Case for Marriage*. New York: Doubleday.

Some Other
New Harbinger Titles

Helping A Child with Nonverbal Learning Disorder, 2nd edition, Item 5266 $15.95

The Introvert & Extrovert in Love, Item 4863 $14.95

Helping Your Socially Vulnerable Child, Item 4580 $15.95

Life Planning for Adults with Developmental Disabilities, Item 4511 $19.95

But I Didn't Mean That! Item 4887 $14.95

The Family Intervention Guide to Mental Illness, Item 5068 $17.95

It's So Hard to Love You, Item 4962 $14.95

The Turbulent Twenties, Item 4216 $14.95

The Balanced Mom, Item 4534 $14.95

Helping Your Child Overcome Separation Anxiety & School Refusal, Item 4313 $14.95

When Your Child Is Cutting, Item 4375 $15.95

Helping Your Child with Selective Mutism, Item 416X $14.95

Sun Protection for Life, Item 4194 $11.95

Helping Your Child with Autism Spectrum Disorder, Item 3848 $17.95

Teach Me to Say It Right, Item 4038 $13.95

Grieving Mindfully, Item 4011 $14.95

The Courage to Trust, Item 3805 $14.95

The Gift of ADHD, Item 3899 $14.95

The Power of Two Workbook, Item 3341 $19.95

Adult Children of Divorce, Item 3368 $14.95

Fifty Great Tips, Tricks, and Techniques to Connect with Your Teen, Item 3597 $10.95

Helping Your Child with OCD, Item 3325 $19.95

Helping Your Depressed Child, Item 3228 $14.95

The Couples's Guide to Love and Money, Item 3112 $18.95

50 Wonderful Ways to be a Single-Parent Family, Item 3082 $12.95

Caring for Your Grieving Child, Item 3066 $14.95

Helping Your Child Overcome an Eating Disorder, Item 3104 $16.95

Helping Your Angry Child, Item 3120 $19.95

The Stepparent's Survival Guide, Item 3058 $17.95

Drugs and Your Kid, Item 3015 $15.95

The Daughter-In-Law's Survival Guide, Item 2817 $12.95

Whose Life Is It Anyway?, Item 2892 $14.95

Call **toll free, 1-800-748-6273,** or log on to our online bookstore at **www.newharbinger.com** to order. Have your Visa or Mastercard number ready. Or send a check for the titles you want to New Harbinger Publications, Inc., 5674 Shattuck Ave., Oakland, CA 94609. Include $4.50 for the first book and 75¢ for each additional book, to cover shipping and handling. (California residents please include appropriate sales tax.) Allow two to five weeks for delivery.

Prices subject to change without notice.